YALE ROMANIC STUDIES: *Second Series*

I

AGRIPPA D'AUBIGNÉ'S *LES TRAGIQUES*

AMS PRESS
NEW YORK

Agrippa d'Aubigné's *Les Tragiques*

A STUDY OF THE BAROQUE STYLE IN POETRY

BY IMBRIE BUFFUM

NEW HAVEN : YALE UNIVERSITY PRESS : 1951

Paris · Presses Universitaires de France

Library of Congress Cataloging in Publication Data

Buffum, Imbrie, 1915-
    Agrippa d'Aubigne's Les tragiques.

    Reprint of the 1951 ed. published by the Yale
University Press, New Haven, which was issued as no. 1
in the second series of Yale Romantic studies.
    Bibliography: p.
    1. Aubigne, Theodore Agrippa d', 1552-1630.
Les tragiques. 2. Baroque literature—History and
criticism. 3. French literature—16th century—History
and criticism. I. Title. II. Series: Yale Romantic
studies; 2d ser., 1.
[PQ1603.A73B8 1978   841'.3   75-41042
ISBN 0-404-14804-2

ACKNOWLEDGMENTS

IN THE SPRING of 1947 Professor René Wellek gave a lecture before the Romance Journal Club of Yale on "The Concept of the Baroque in Literary Scholarship." A few months earlier I had become interested in d'Aubigné; I felt that the traditional evaluation of this poet as a "retardataire et égaré" was unjust and patronizing. As I listened to Professor Wellek it occurred to me that d'Aubigné's description of the Massacre of St. Bartholomew did indeed have many points in common with baroque painting. This idea is the origin of my book.

For the transformation of the idea into a book I am indebted to Professor Henri Peyre of the Yale French Department. Professor Peyre's stimulating advice on problems of method, organization, and style and above all his sympathetic interest have made it possible for me to carry out my original idea. I am also most grateful to him for his efforts in arranging the actual publication.

It is my hope that the present study may lead more students of French literature to the love and understanding of a strange poet.

IMBRIE BUFFUM

Silliman College
Yale University
May 1951

CONTENTS

INTRODUCTION

It is the aim of this book to present the *Tragiques* of Agrippa d'Aubigné as an example of the baroque style in poetry. Since the study rests upon several basic assumptions, it is well that these should be explained to the reader at the outset.

1. First of all, I believe, with the poet's biographer, Rocheblave, that d'Aubigné, better perhaps than any of his contemporaries, represents the spirit of his time. The poet's life span extends from 1552 to 1630: this is the period which, in the plastic arts of Europe, is characterized by the baroque style. Historians of French letters have been somewhat embarrassed to give a name to this epoch, which links the Renaissance to classicism, and as a result have generally been obliged to term it an age of transition. The eight religious wars of sixteenth-century France are contained within this lifetime; for more than thirty years d'Aubigné himself was a soldier, fighting and risking his life for the Protestant cause. He was frequently wounded, sometimes a prisoner, and narrowly escaped being a victim of the Massacre of St. Bartholomew, which took place when he was a young man of twenty.

Combining as he does humanism, fanatical belief, and violent action d'Aubigné seems exceptionally well fitted to represent the transition from the sixteenth to the seventeenth century. It is true that the literary figure who dominates these years is Montaigne; but the author of the *Essais,* though in many ways providing a bridge from Renaissance to classicism, is, by virtue of his detachment and philosophical moderation, hardly typical of a passionate epoch. And even as a humanist d'Aubigné almost bears comparison with Montaigne. Although Jean d'Aubigné, unlike Pierre Eyquem, did not teach his son to speak Latin before he spoke French, nevertheless young Agrippa, at the age of six, was able to read Latin, Greek, and Hebrew, and at seven and a half to make a translation of Plato's *Crito.* The father had been converted to the Protestant faith shortly before the son's birth and had, as a result, lost his position as judge at Pons in Saintonge. Jean d'Aubigné evidently rose rapidly to a position of power in the Protestant party, for when, eleven years later, he died of wounds received in battle he had already become the chancellor of the king of Navarre.

It is natural that such a man should be strong in his determination to make his son a fanatical fighter for the reformed faith. In the poet's ninth year, the two were passing through Amboise on their way to Paris; the decapitated heads of the leaders of the famous Protestant conspiracy were publicly displayed on a gallows. The father turned to the boy and made him take an oath of loyalty to the Protestant cause, saying: "My son, your head must not be spared after mine, to avenge these glorious leaders; if you shirk this duty, you will have my curse." The lesson was not lost on Agrippa who, a few years later, locked in his room by relatives who wished to protect him from his own impetuousness, escaped by a sheet-ladder in order to join the Protestant army in the Second Religious War. This was the beginning of a military career which lasted, almost without interruption, for three decades. We may gain some idea of the brutal excesses to which d'Aubigné's religious fanaticism drove him from an episode related in his *Vie à ses enfans.* Once at the age of twenty, lying wounded and believing that he was on his deathbed, he shouted his final confession aloud. So horrifying (he maintains) was the list of crimes that the attendant soldiers' hair stood on end.

In the field of action, d'Aubigné's decisive contribution to history is the influence he exerted on his inseparable companion and chief, the king of Navarre, later to become Henri IV of France. The association of these two Protestant warriors lasted for fifteen years, ending only with the king's abjuration of the reformed faith. On three occasions at least Agrippa strengthened Henri's will in a critical moment and thereby determined the future history of France. One night in 1576, when Henri de Navarre was tossing in his bed in the Louvre, a virtual prisoner of Catherine de' Medici, d'Aubigné brusquely opened the curtains and addressed him in these words:

Your Majesty, is it true that the spirit of God is still working and dwelling in you? You are sighing to God for the absence of your friends and faithful servants, and at the same time they are together sighing for yours and working for your freedom: but you have only tears in your eyes, and they have arms in their hands. They are fighting your enemies, and you are serving them. . . . They fear only God, you a woman, Catherine . . . they are on horseback, and you are on your knees. . . .

Henri, shamed by the outspoken courage of his tireless and loyal ambassador, was roused from his indecision and made good his escape to the Protestant armies.

At another moment in history, when the death of the Duke of Alençon had made Henri the heir presumptive to the throne of France, there was again vacillation among the Protestants, some of whom favored a policy of disbanding their armies and infiltrating the forces of the Ligue. It was a passionate oration by d'Aubigné that convinced the king and his followers of the dangers of appeasement and the necessity of maintaining their military strength. Finally, if we may believe the *Vie à ses enfans,* when Henri III lay assassinated and the future Henri IV stood at his bier, frightened by the angry opposition of Catholic leaders, only a forceful speech by d'Aubigné gave him the courage to assert himself as the rightful king.

2. A second assumption has been made in this study of *Les Tragiques:* it is the conviction that d'Aubigné's principal literary work forms a parallel to the actions of his life. His pen fights the same battle as his sword. The book exhibits the same tendencies toward fanaticism, violence, and sadism as the man. In *Les Tragiques,* as in the thirty years of his career as a soldier, he devotes all the energies of a fiery spirit to waging war upon his enemies: Catherine de' Medici, the degenerate Valois kings, the hated foreigners who devastate France, the corrupt law courts, the Guises, the Inquisition, the Catholic Church. Just as, in actual life, the role of d'Aubigné was to rouse the flagging spirits of his fellow Protestants, so the function of *Les Tragiques* is to restore and maintain the vigor of their faith after defeat. If, as a man, d'Aubigné is typical of the spirit of his age, he is no less so as a poet.

In the intimate autobiography which d'Aubigné wrote for his children, he has chosen chiefly to record the dramatic and forceful retorts which he made at various significant moments of his life. These striking speeches bear an interesting resemblance to the literary style of *Les Tragiques* and constitute further evidence of the parallel between d'Aubigné's life and his poetry. When, for example, the youthful d'Aubigné was a prisoner of the Catholics, who threatened him with burning at the stake, he replied that "l'horreur de la Messe luy ostoit celle du feu." Upon another occasion, a Catholic nobleman offered him a huge bribe to surrender confidential documents implicating certain important Protestants in the Amboise Conspiracy. D'Aubigné disappeared for a moment and then returned with a large velvet bag. This, in the presence of his tempter, he threw into the fire, saying "Je les ay bruslees de peur qu'elles ne me bruslassent, car j'avoys pensé à la tentation." The poet's speech to the captive king in the Louvre has already been mentioned as an illustration of the active part he played in history; but it is no less interesting, with its antitheses and metaphors, as an example of d'Aubigné's language: the style is recognizable to anyone familiar with *Les Tragiques.* Of all the memorable remonstrances to Henri of Navarre, however, none bears the mark of the poet's style more vividly than these bitter and prophetic words, spoken after the king had received a wound in the mouth: "Sire, vous n'avez renié Dieu que des lèvres, il s'est contenté de les percer; quand vous le renierez du cœur, il percera le cœur." The memory of this bold sally must have given the speaker grim satisfaction when, years later in retirement in Geneva, he learned of the assassination of Henri IV. D'Aubigné was always eager to discover, in the disasters of history, evidences of divine retribution. The sixth book of *Les Tragiques,* characteristically entitled *Vengeances,* lists the punishments inflicted by God upon the wicked throughout the ages; the poet hopes that a similar doom awaits the Catholics.

3. Implicit in this importance attached to the memorable sayings of d'Aubigné's life is a third assumption: that style and spirit are related. For in the analysis of *Les Tragiques* I am studying not only the baroque style but also the baroque spirit. It is my contention that the habitual use of certain stylistic devices reveals a certain way of looking at life. In making *mots historiques* at critical moments in his career, d'Aubigné employs various rhetorical figures which we shall see in *Les Tragiques* itself: exaggeration, asyndeton, the echo device, concrete imagery, metaphoric antithesis and contrast, to name only a few. If such devices were to be met with in the poem alone and not in the actual speech of his life, it might be argued that d'Aubigné is merely following literary conventions and not yielding to fundamental impulses of his nature. I believe, however, that form and content are interrelated, and that the poet, in choosing certain forms, is expressing his inner spirit. Taking the spirit of d'Aubigné to be representative of his age as I do, I see the stylistic devices employed in *Les Tragiques* not as artificial and external but as of fundamental importance for the understanding both of this particular poet and of the baroque age in general.

4. The fourth assumption is that there exist stylistic parallels between the literature of an age and its painting, sculpture, and architecture. Characteristics of technique or spirit to be discovered in the fine arts of a period are likely to be reflected in its literature. Consequently, in this study, I have felt it justifiable and pertinent to call attention to similarities, whether of form or of content, between *Les Tragiques* and the works of such artists as Bernini, Tintoretto, or El Greco. This method has perhaps not frequently been used in analyses of French literature of the late sixteenth and early seventeenth centuries; the procedure, however, appears to be fairly well established with respect to writers of other periods. Huizinga, for example, in his *Waning of the Middle Ages,* has shown the connection between the *danses macabres* of the fifteenth century and the poetry of François Villon. What teacher, in endeavoring to communicate to his students the orderly beauty of French classical tragedy, has not had recourse, for the purposes of comparison, to photographs of the gardens of Lenôtre at Versailles? Similarly, a study of the paintings of Watteau, with their mixture of wistful tenderness and gaiety, will contribute much toward the understanding of the spirit of Marivaux: to appreciate the style and spirit of the "Embarkation for Cytherea" is to appreciate *Le Jeu de l'amour et du hasard* or *Les Fausses Confidences.* And finally, it will readily be conceded that there exists much parallelism of subject matter, aim, and technique between the painting of Monet, Pisarro, or Sisley and the poetry of Verlaine.

Although *Les Tragiques* was not completed and published until 1616, much of the poem was actually composed in the heat of the religious wars, during the closing decades of the sixteenth century. As we survey the field of the fine arts we find that the period generally considered as baroque extends from the 1530's until the latter half of the seventeenth century. Michelangelo's "Last Judgment," in the Sistine Chapel, is probably the ancestor of all baroque art; the master worked upon it from 1534 to 1541. The life spans of two important baroque artists include, either in whole or in part, the years during which d'Aubigné was writing his poem: Tintoretto (1512–94) and Rubens (1577–1640). Two of the most celebrated baroque works date from approximately the same period as the composition of *Les Tragiques:* El Greco's "Burial of Count Orgaz" (1584) and Maderna's façade of St. Peter's in Rome (1607–14). It will probably be remarked that, in the course of this study, parallels are constantly drawn between the art of d'Aubigné and that of Italian, Spanish, or even Flemish contemporaries but relative silence is observed on the subject of French artists. It must indeed be admitted that, while the baroque style dominates the painting, sculpture, and architecture of most of Europe at the turn of the century, it does not appear to affect these arts in France until somewhat later, and then only to a lesser degree. The painters Simon Vouet (1590–1649) and Georges de la Tour (1600–1652) may perhaps be regarded as moderately baroque; the first baroque building in Paris, the Church of St.-Joseph-des-Carmes, was begun in 1613; other examples of the style, such as the Val-de-Grâce (1645–67) and the Invalides (1671–1706) are not very numerous. However, there appear to be striking parallels between *Les Tragiques* and the baroque of other countries; in France d'Aubigné is a precursor. It should further be emphasized that elsewhere in Europe the baroque continues to flourish for many years after the publication of *Les Tragiques:* Bernini's masterpiece, "Santa Teresa," dates from 1646, and Murillo lived until 1682.

5. The fifth and final assumption is suggested by much that precedes. I believe that the baroque is an independent and recognizable style, worthy of study and admiration for its own sake, neither a "decadent" form of Renaissance art nor merely a "transitional" style. Toward the end of the nineteenth century there began to occur among scholars and critics a significant revival of interest in the baroque. This rehabilitation of an unjustly scorned style was largely due to the efforts of the Swiss art historian Heinrich Wölfflin, whose two epoch-making works, *Renaissance and Baroque* (1888) and *Principles of Art History* (1915) did much to change the popular conception that the baroque was simply a degenerate form of Renaissance art, and also helped establish precise criteria for the identification of the baroque style in painting, architecture, and sculpture. Other important scholarly works which reflect the

reorientation of taste are Werner Weisbach's *Der Barock als Kunst der Gegenreformation* (1922) and Emile Mâle's *L'Art religieux après le Concile de Trente* (1932). The latter work, indeed, coming from a scholar whose principal field of activity had hitherto been the Middle Ages, represents a significant departure. However, the works of both Mâle and Weisbach are more concerned with iconography and subject matter than with style and technique. Both tend to identify the baroque with the Counter Reformation, particularly with the Jesuits, and stress such aspects as religious propaganda, the depiction of horror and martyrdom, or the concern with vision and ecstasy. For determining the essential characteristics of the baroque style in the fine arts, Wölfflin's famous categories (linear vs. painterly, plane vs. recession, closed vs. open form, multiplicity vs. unity, clearness vs. unclearness) remain the most valid criteria. Viewed in the light of these standards, such a northern and Protestant artist as Rembrandt may, by virtue of his stylistic peculiarities, be considered baroque. The baroque style, while corresponding to a particular period in history, transcends national and religious boundaries.

In recent years literary historians have grown aware of a similar problem in their own field. René Wellek, in an extremely important article, "The Concept of the Baroque in Literary Scholarship," has traced the history of the word "baroque" as a term of *literary* criticism, and has compiled a comprehensive bibliography of the subject from 1888 to 1946. He points out that the term has met with varying degrees of acceptance in different countries: ". . . its complete establishment in Germany, its recent success in Italy and Spain, its slow penetration into English and American scholarship, and its almost complete failure in France." It must indeed be confessed that, faced with this concept, most French scholars prove refractory; their reluctance may in part be explained by the pejorative connotations of the word in the French language and in part by the fact that the idea tends to impinge upon the sacrosanct category of classicism. Mr. Wellek goes on to discuss the various problems raised by the concept; some critics "use baroque as a term for a recurrent phenomenon in all history and [some] . . . use it as a term for a specific phenomenon in the historical phenomenon, fixed in time and place." Two examples of these opposing attitudes would be Eugenio d'Ors, who sees baroque throughout human history and indeed in all literary or artistic works not governed by intellectual abstraction and rigid classicism, and, on the other hand, the view expressed in Austin Warren's *Richard Crashaw,* where baroque sensibility is closely related to the Catholicism of the late sixteenth and early seventeenth centuries. Furthermore, in Mr. Wellek's words, "baroque can be used pejoratively, or as a neutral descriptive term, or as a term of praise." Finally, the most important question remains: "What is the precise content of the word baroque?" Mr. Wellek deprecates the transference of Wölfflin's criteria to literature, and also feels that any attempt to define the baroque in terms of stylistic devices is attended with grave difficulty, inasmuch as all such devices are to be encountered at widely separated moments of literary history. He similarly indicates the dangers of attempting to connect the baroque with a "philosophy or a world-view or even a merely emotional attitude toward the world" (as in Gonzague de Reynold's idea that the baroque spirit is strong-willed and pessimistic, Eugenio d'Ors's pantheism, or the "antithetical feeling of life" discerned by certain German critics). The conclusion of Mr. Wellek's article is that "the most promising way of arriving at a more closely fitting description of the baroque is to aim at analyses which would correlate stylistic and ideological criteria." It is this last method which has been the guiding principle of the present study.

The intention in this book is to examine in detail a specific literary work by a specific author belonging to that period which art historians have accepted as baroque. I shall attempt to analyze the salient features of this poem with regard to both subject matter and style, both form and content. In other words, I shall begin by observing precise phenomena which may actually be seen in a definite work; the method is a posteriori rather than a priori, inductive rather than deductive. In studying these aspects of form and content, I shall endeavor to see whether any relationship exists between various apparently separate characteristics—in short, whether a *coherent style* may be found in *Les Tragiques.* Since individual devices may exist at all stages of the history of literature, a recognizable style is likely to exist only if the devices exist in some sort of conjunction. When, in the course of this book, I have occasion to describe some rhetorical figure as baroque I am not arguing that its presence alone constitutes proof of this style. The accumulation of a wide *variety* of such evidence is essential. An attempt will be made to discover whether a recognizable spirit underlies the phenomena of form and content observed.

Chapter I: ENERGY

IT HAS frequently been remarked that the painting and sculpture of the baroque period are animated by a spirit of propaganda; art is made to serve a religious or moral purpose. In the years following the Counter Reformation the Catholic Church used art to further her struggle against Protestantism. Emile Mâle has pointed out, in his exhaustive study of iconography, *L'Art religieux après le Concile de Trente,* how the plastic arts undertook to defend all the varied dogmas, forms of worship, and institutions which had been attacked by the Protestants. For example, the Reformation had assailed the worship of images, and thus we see Baglione, in his frescoes at Santa Maria Maggiore, depicting the violent deaths of iconoclastic emperors. The Protestants were especially hostile to the cult of the Virgin; Catholic art of the late sixteenth and seventeenth centuries has, as one of its main themes, the exaltation of the Virgin. In Naples Cathedral Domenichino depicted the triumph of the Virgin over Protestantism; the fresco shows Mary enthroned upon a cloud, while a young athlete tramples Luther and Calvin underfoot. It was during the Counter Reformation that the belief in the Immaculate Conception was proclaimed and found its most ardent champions among the Jesuits. Spanish art, in particular, was fond of the subject; perhaps no artist has treated it more frequently or more brilliantly than Murillo, whose many versions, in the Louvre, Prado, and elsewhere, immediately come to mind.

The institution of the papacy was the object of the fiercest attacks of the Protestants; some of the greatest baroque masterpieces were called into being to illustrate and defend it. The façade of St. Peter's in Rome, which was completed in 1612, exists primarily for the purpose of proclaiming the glory of the papacy; by its size and magnificence it impresses the beholder with the power of the Roman church. The single bas-relief on this façade, furthermore, shows Christ giving the keys to St. Peter; the divine origin of the Church is thereby affirmed. One of the most spectacular works in the interior is Bernini's monument of the Cathedra Petri. As Mâle points out, it is precisely because the Protestants had challenged the legitimacy of the successors of St. Peter that in the latter half of the sixteenth century it was felt necessary to employ one of the greatest artists to enshrine the throne of the "Prince of the Apostles."

Other beliefs were likewise being threatened; for example, the reality of purgatory was denied by the Protestants. Consequently, many pictures were devoted to this subject: Guercino has a fine painting of St. Gregory and the souls in purgatory (in the Church of San Paolo in Bologna), and Philippe de Champagne represents Christ and the Virgin consoling them (Toulouse Museum). Among the sacraments rejected by the Reformation is that of penance. Once again we see the Counter Reformation artists defending it, as in Guido Reni's "Repentance of St. Peter," Ribera's "Penitent Mary Magdalene," or Rubens' "Sinners Saved by Repentance." (It is, in large part, this desire to illustrate the sacrament of penance which explains the great popularity, in this period, of the Magdalene as a subject.) The most important sacrament rejected by the Protestants was that of the Eucharist; and here we have a host of great pictures inspired by the desire to make the beholder believe in its reality: Ribera's "Christ Giving Communion to the Apostles," Rubens' "Christ Consecrating the Bread and the Wine," Domenichino's "Last Communion of St. Jerome," and many others. Particularly spectacular and baroque in spirit is Rubens' "Triumph of the Eucharist" in the Prado: one scene depicts a throng of pagan priests, with their intended sacrificial victim, put to disorderly rout by the appearance of an angel brandishing a chalice; another scene shows Religion riding in triumph in a golden chariot while holding aloft the Eucharist for the adoration of the multitude.

Another series of Catholic paintings glorifies those saints, such as St. Charles Borromeo or St. Teresa, who are famous for their good works or their missionary activity. The Church felt it necessary to honor these heroes because Luther and Calvin had denied the importance of good works and had taught the doctrine of salvation through faith alone. Thus, when Murillo paints St. Elizabeth, the queen of Portugal, caring for the sick,[1] or St. Thomas of Villeneuve giving alms to the poor,[2] he is using art for a propaganda purpose.

It would seem, then, that in much of the painting and sculpture of the baroque period beauty is made to serve the artist's conception of truth. If we turn to poetry and look at the works of that poet most generally conceded by critics to be baroque—Crashaw—we find that he too is using his art for a religious purpose. Indeed, many of his subjects are the same as those chosen by Murillo or Bernini: for example, "In the Glorious Assumption of Our Blessed Lady," "Saint Mary Magdalene or the Weeper," and "Hymn to Saint Teresa." Other baroque themes include "Sancta Maria Dolorum," a "Hymn for the Blessed Sacrament," and a "Hymn to the Name of Jesus." It would be a mistake to disparage the technical skill of Crashaw, but it is nevertheless evident that this skill is merely a means to an end and that this end is to win converts to a religious faith. Nothing could be farther from Crashaw's mind than the

1. In the Prado, Madrid.
2. Provincial Museum, Seville. The paintings mentioned here are reproduced in Mâle, *L'Art religieux*.

concept of art for art's sake; the purpose of his poetry is to glorify the Catholic religion.

It should not be thought, however, that this missionary aspect of baroque art and poetry is an exclusively Catholic phenomenon. Because of the important connection between the Counter Reformation and the art of the period, some critics have sought to identify the baroque with Catholicism. To do so is an undue restriction of the concept. To be sure, the Protestants' disapproval of images made them loath to use the plastic arts as a means of spreading their beliefs, but they never hesitated to make poetry serve their cause. The *Holy Sonnets* of John Donne and *Paradise Lost* are outstanding examples of poetry in the service of Protestantism. Indeed Milton, in the opening lines of his poem, proclaims his religious purpose. His intention is to

> . . . assert Eternal Providence
> And justify the ways of God to men.

The spirit of propaganda in art, being one manifestation of the baroque style, transcends the boundaries of any single country or religion; artists who lived at the end of the sixteenth or in the seventeenth century quite naturally used their skill to further the causes in which they believed.

This is the purpose which animates d'Aubigné's *Tragiques*. In his introduction to the reader, the author explicitly states that he has in view a religious and moral end:

> La matière de l'œuvre a pour sept livres sept titres separez, qui toutefois ont quelque convenance, comme des effects aux causes. Le premier livre s'appelle *Misères*, qui est un tableau piteux du Royaume en general, d'un style bas et tragique, n'excedant que fort peu les loix de la narration. Les *Princes* viennent après, d'un style moyen mais satyrique en quelque façon: en cettui-là il a esgallé la liberté de ces escrits à celles des vices de son temps, denotant le subject de ce second pour instrument du premier. Et puis il fait contribuer aux causes des miseres l'injustice, sous le titre de *La Chambre dorée*, mais ce troisiesme de mesme style que le second. Le quart, qu'il appelle *Les Feux*, est tout entier au sentiment de la religion de l'autheur et d'un style tragicque moyen. Le cinquiesme, sous le nom des *Fers*, du style tragicque eslevé, plus poëtic et plus hardi que les autres. . . . Le livre qui suit le cinquiesme s'appelle *Vengeances*, théologien et historial. Lui et le dernier, qui est le *Jugement*, d'un style eslevé, tragicque, pourront estre blasmés pour la passion partizane; mais ce genre d'escrire a pour but d'esmouvoir, et l'autheur le tient quitte s'il peut cela sur les esprits desjà passionnez ou pour le moins aequanimes.[3]

The poetic form, in other words, is a vehicle for moral, political, and religious convictions. It is d'Aubigné's intent to move the reader and to reform France. In *Misères* he seeks to arouse pity for the condition of his country and

---

3. *Les Tragiques*, "Aux Lecteurs," p. 9.

to convince us of the horrors of civil war; in the next two books respectively he expresses indignation at the immorality of the king and the corruption of the law courts; in *Les Feux* and *Les Fers* he passionately pleads the cause of the Protestant martyrs; *Vengeances* and *Jugement* are grandiose and forceful presentations of Protestant theology. The poet is well aware of the fact that he is open to the charge of fanaticism but frankly admits that his purpose is to arouse the reader's emotions.

D'Aubigné's moral aim also finds expression in the verse preface to *Les Tragiques*. With excessive and probably not altogether sincere modesty, he compares his poem to a rudely clad Danubian peasant uttering unpleasant but salutary truths:

> Sois hardi, ne te cache point,
> Entre chez les Rois mal en point;
> Que la pauvreté de ta robbe
> Ne te face honte ni peur,
> Ne te diminuë ou desrobe
> La suffisance ni le cœur.
> Porte, comme au senat romain,
> L'advis & l'habit du vilain
> Qui vint du Danube sauvage,
> Et monstra hideux, effronté,
> De la façon non du langage,
> La mal-plaisante verité.[4]

If the poet were interested in writing poetry for its own sake, if he were concerned primarily with the rhythmic creation of beauty, one of his principal concerns would be *to please;* but since he is animated by the spirit of propaganda he has a great desire to command attention by shocking; he actually takes pleasure in *displeasing:*

> Si mon esprit audacieux
> Veut peindre le secret des cieux
> J'attaque les Dieux de la terre:
> Il faut bien qu'il me soit permis
> De fouiller, pour leur faire guerre,
> L'arcenal de leurs ennemis.
> Je n'excuse pas mes escrits
> Pour ceux-là qui y sont repris:
> Mon plaisir est de leur desplaire.
> Amis, je trouve en la raison
> Pour vous & pour eux fruict contraire,
> La medecine & le poison.[5]

4. *Préface*, 13–24.
5. *Préface*, 361–372.

Since d'Aubigné was all his life an active soldier in the Protestant cause, it is natural that his poetic propaganda should express itself in military images—"attacking," "making war," and "arsenal." Violence of vocabulary is a significant aspect of the baroque style and merits detailed study elsewhere. It should be noted here, however, that religious zealots tend to think in military terms (as witness the organization of the Jesuit order) and that images such as the above are a logical consequence of the missionary spirit. The idea that *Les Tragiques* are to be a poison to some and a medicine to others is further evidence of d'Aubigné's reform intentions.

The theme of attack, with its concomitant military imagery, reappears in the very first line of *Misères,* where the poet declares that he is going to attack the Roman legions. Early in the same book the author of the *Printemps* renounces love poetry and dedicates himself to the higher causes of patriotism and religion. There is a note of contempt as he refers to the writings of his youth, and by implication this scorn extends to lyric poetry in general:

> Je n'escris plus les feux d'un amour inconu,
> Mais, par l'affliction plus sage devenu,
> I'entreprens bien plus haut, car j'apprens à ma plume
> Un autre feu, auquel la France se consume.

> Au lieu de Thessalie aux mignardes vallées
> Nous avortons ces chants au milieu des armées,

> Le luth que j'accordois avec mes chansonnettes
> Est ores estouffé de l'esclat des trompettes; [6]

The doctrine here suggested is that the value of a poem depends upon its moral earnestness; questionable as this critical theory may be it reveals much as to d'Aubigné's conception of the nature and purpose of poetry.

Being a stern moralist who is genuinely afflicted by the misery of France, d'Aubigné does not hesitate to assign blame to those in authority: diatribes are frequent throughout the *Tragiques* and especially in the *Misères.* Long passages of violent denunciation are, indeed, inevitable in a work so motivated by partisanship and the spirit of propaganda, and it is often in such passages that the author's poetic power is most apparent. The sincerity of the poet's indignation is unmistakable as he begins his black list:

> Financiers, justiciers, qui opprimez de faim
> Celui qui vous fait naistre ou qui defend le pain,
> Sous qui le laboureur s'abreuve de ses larmes, [7]

> Barbares en effect, François de nom, François,
> Vos fausses lois ont fait des faux & jeunes Rois,

6. *Misères,* 55–74, *passim.*
7. *Misères,* 163–165.

Impuissans sur leurs coeurs, cruels en leur puissance; [8]

Mes cheveux estonnez herissent en ma teste;
J'appelle Dieu pour juge, & tout haut je deteste
Les violeurs de paix, les perfides parfaicts
Qui d'une salle cause amenent tels effects.[9]

Et encore aujourd'hui, sous la loi de la guerre,
Les tygres vont bruslans les thresors de la terre,[10]

Judges, financiers, military leaders, the king's ministers—d'Aubigné spares
none of those whom he feels to be responsible; in fact, as we shall see elsewhere, the higher the rank of the offender the more terrible is the poet's wrath.
The comparison between the kings of the good old days, beloved of their subjects and welcomed with affection whenever they made triumphal entries, and
the modern tyrants who terrify the city dwellers by their approach is scarcely
flattering to the Valois rulers:

Nos tyrans aujourd'hui entrent d'une autre sorte,
La ville qui les void a visage de morte.
Quand son prince la foulle, il la void de tels yeux
Que Neron voyoit Romm' en l'esclat de ses feux; [11]

The full force of the prophet's anger, however, is reserved for Catherine de'
Medici and the Cardinal of Lorraine; it is when he is denouncing these two
that his accents most resemble those of a Jeremiah:

Voici les deux flambeaux & les deux instruments
Des playes de la France, & de tous ses tourments:
Une fatale femme, un cardinal qui d'elle,
Parangon de mal-heur, suivoit l'ame cruelle,[12]

Catherine becomes Jezebel; this epithet, it is true, was not original with
d'Aubigné but fairly general among the Hugenots; d'Aubigné's hatred, however, gives the term fresh vitality:

Pleust à Dieu, Jesabel, que tu euss'à Florence
Laissé tes trahisons, en laissant ton païs,
Que tu n'eusse les grands des deux costez trahis
Pour regner au milieu, & que ton entreprise
N'eust ruiné le noble & le peuple & l'Eglise!
Cinq cens mille soldats n'eussent crevé, poudreux,
Sur le champ maternel, & ne fust avec eux

8. *Misères*, 191–193.
9. *Misères*, 429–432.
10. *Misères*, 437–438.
11. *Misères*, 581–584.
12. *Misères*, 723–726.

> La noblesse faillie & la force faillie
> De France, que tu as faict gibier d'Italie.[13]

Over two hundred lines of invective are devoted to the queen mother's sins, and the tone of violence is maintained throughout. As might be expected, the pope is another special target of abuse. He is called the "beast of Rome" and the "Roman wolf"; he is worse than Nero ever was. D'Aubigné particularly resents the submission of French kings to papal domination:

> . . . on void, sans qu'on s'estonne
> La pantoufle crotter les lys de la couronne: [14]

The overweaning arrogance of the pope is denounced, and the following words are put in his mouth:

> "Je dispense, dit-il, du droict contre le droict;
> Celui que j'ai damné, quand le ciel le voudroit,
> Ne peut estre sauvé; j'authorise le vice;
> Je fai le faict non faict, de justice injustice;
> Je sauve les damnez en un petit moment;
> J'en loge dans le ciel à coup un regiment;
> Je fai de bouë un Roy, je mets les Rois aux fanges;
> Je fai les Saincts, sous moy obeïssent les Anges;
> Je puis (cause première à tout cet univers)
> Mettre l'enfer au ciel & le ciel aux enfers." [15]

This theory of the papal authority is ascribed to the Jesuits, who are attacked as "Spanish vermin," usurpers of the name of Jesus, who hide daggers under their cloaks and spread hell-fire throughout Europe.

The foregoing examples are from *Misères,* but one could proceed through the other six books and see everywhere the determination of the poet to fight the enemies of his religion. *Princes* opens with an emphatic declaration of moral intent: vice is to be exposed, and whited sepulchers opened wherever they may be and however horrible the stench. Addressing the dissolute princes, d'Aubigné summons them to contemplate the horror of their own lives:

> Lisez-le: vous aurez horreur de vostre horreur!
> Non pas que j'aye espoir qu'une pudique honte
> Vos pasles fronts de chien par vergogne surmonte; [16]

The poet then declares that the corruption of the court is Goliath, that he is David, and that the enemy shall die. The second book of the *Tragiques* is generally considered to be satirical rather than tragic or epic in tone, and there

13. *Misères,* 758–766.
14. *Misères,* 1217–1218.
15. *Misères,* 1235–1244.
16. *Princes,* 12–14.

is of course much stinging satire in the picture of the effeminate king surrounded by his dissolute favorites; but the sting comes precisely from the
strong moral purpose that underlies the book. It is with the purpose of height-
ening our realization of the dangerous moral example set by the princes that
d'Aubigné has introduced his story of the arrival at court of an innocent young
man. In the peroration which closes the book, satire is dropped in favor of
exhortation:

> Fuyez, Loths, de Sodome & Gomorrhe bruslantes,
> N'ensevelissez pas vos ames innocentes
> Avec ces reprouvez; . . .[17]

The satire of the law courts in *La Chambre dorée* likewise derives its power
from the zeal of a reformer. The labored allegory which occupies so large a
part of the book is scarcely justifiable on artistic grounds, and is an example
of the literary excesses which can result from a predilection for moralizing.
The exhortation to the wicked judges in the closing lines forms a parallel to
the appeal to the princes at the beginning of the preceding book:

> Lisez, persecuteurs, le reste de mes chants,
> Vous y pourrez gouster le breuvage aux meschants:
> Mais, aspics, vous avez pour moy l'oreille close.[18]

And d'Aubigné then paraphrases a psalm of David directed at evil judges.
The spirit of fanaticism tends to result in self-identification with the Deity,
and the author of the *Tragiques* is not always innocent of this. He is wont to
appeal to God for inspiration, as in the following passage from *Les Feux,* just
before he undertakes his long catalogue of Protestant martyrs:

> Condui mon œuvre, ô Dieu, à ton nom, donne moy
> Qu'entre tant de martyrs, champions de la foy,
> De chasque sexe, estat ou aage, à ton sainct temple
> Je puisse consacrer un tableau pour exemple.[19]

It is natural for the poet, going a step further, to assume that his prayers for
guidance have been granted and that he has actually become the mouthpiece
of God. Presumably it is this conviction which gives him the confidence to
preach sermons even to the leader of the Protestants, Henri of Navarre:

> Henri, qui tous les jours vas prodiguant ta vie,
> Pour remettre le regne, oster la tyrannie,
> Ennemi des tyrans, ressource des vrais Rois,
> Quand les sceptre des lis joindra le Navarrois,

17. *Princes*, 1503–1505.
18. *La Chambre dorée*, 1001–1003.
19. *Les Feux*, 19–22.

Souvien-toi de quel œil, de quelle vigilance,
Tu vois & remedie aux mal-heurs de la France;
Souvien-toy quelque jour combien sont ignorans
Ceux qui pour estre Rois veulent estre tyrans.[20]

In the great appeal to France personified, which comes immediately after the
admonition to Henri, d'Aubigné is once more playing the part of the prophet;
and indeed throughout *Les Tragiques* he seems certain that he is expressing
the will of God. This spirit of propaganda, fully as much as the numerous
borrowings from biblical style, is reminiscent of Jeremiah or Isaiah. One
passage from *Les Fers* is very revealing as to the conception he had of his
poetry:

Tu m'as montré, ô Dieu, que celuy qui te sert
Sauve sa vie alors que pour toy il la perd:
Ta main m'a délivré, je te sacre la mienne,
Je remets en ton sein cette ame qui est tienne.
Tu m'as donné la voix, je te louërai, mon Dieu,
Je chanteray ton los & ta force au milieu
De tes sacrés parvis, je feray tes merveilles,
Ta deffence & tes coups retentir aux oreilles
Des princes de la terre, & si le peuple bas
Sçaura par moy comment les tyrans tu abas.[21]

It is clear that d'Aubigné, like El Greco or Milton, felt himself to be in an
intimate personal relationship with God; like them he would be less great if
he did not believe himself to be divinely inspired; like them he was conscious
of fulfilling, through his art, the sacred mission of interpreting God's will to
men. He shares, with the majority of baroque artists in other mediums and
other religious faiths and other countries of western Europe, the conception
that art is a means to the end of glorifying God.

2. DEVICES OF EMPHASIS AND EXAGGERATION

In *Les Tragiques* d'Aubigné produces many of his most striking artistic
effects by overstatement. Whereas in a later generation, under the influence
of Boileau, balance and proportion—extending at times even to understate-
ment—are the order of the day, d'Aubigné likes to express himself with maxi-
mum emphasis. He proceeds by exaggeration rather than by suggestion. In this
respect he produces an impression not unlike the painting, sculpture, and
architecture of his time. The florid, crowded canvasses of a Rubens, the gestur-
ing figures of a Bernini, the imposing, highly decorated façades of Borromini's

20. *Misères*, 593–600.
21. *Les Fers*, 1431–1440.

Roman churches—all these belong to an artistic style which aims at massiveness of effects. It will be worth while, then, to examine in detail a few of the devices of emphasis and exaggeration used in *Les Tragiques*.

A. Asyndeton

One of these devices I shall term asyndeton, though it is my intention here to use the term somewhat loosely. Properly speaking, the word means "a rhetorical figure which omits the conjunction," and even in this sense the device is frequently used by d'Aubigné. However, it seems fitting to consider in this place not only actual asyndeton but also what Hatzfeld has called *Worthäufung* [22]—the heaping-up of words, done constantly throughout *Les Tragiques* for the sake of achieving massiveness and emphasis. In many cases a single adjective, noun, or verb would be sufficient to convey the meaning, but the poet has chosen to be redundant in order to be forceful, adding words to his descriptions as a baroque architect might add columns to a façade. Let us look at some of the examples.

1. *Misères*, 713–714. The French people see an evil portent in a comet foreboding the evil deeds of Catherine de' Medici and the Cardinal of Lorraine. They say:

> . . . "Ce feu menace & promet à la terre,
> Louche, pasle ou flambant, peste, famine, ou guerre."

In order to give heavy emphasis to his hatred of the two public figures whom he believes to be most responsible for the sufferings of the Protestants, the poet has multiplied verbs, adjectives, and nouns. "Threatens" is reinforced by "promises"; the light of the comet is alternately "cloudy," "pale," and "flaming"; it portends "pestilence," "famine," or "war." The extra words add nothing to the essential idea; they are mere decoration.

2. *Misères*, 1253–1254. Imprecations against the Jesuits.

> Allez, preschez, courez, vollez, meurtriere trope,
> Semez le feu d'enfer aux quatre coins d'Europe!

Here, four imperatives are piled up in rapid succession: such an accumulation of verbs, unseparated by connectives, creates an impression of breathless energy.

3. *Princes*, 868. Description of the Duke of Alençon.

> Un sodomite athee, un macquereau, un traistre.

Four insults are stronger than one.

22. H. Hatzfeld, "Der Barockstil der religiösen klassischen Lyrik in Frankreich."

4. *Princes,* 1229-1230. Barbarous treatment of the Protestant leader and
hero, Coligny.

> L'Amiral pour jamais sans surnom, trop connu,
> Meurtri, précipité, traisné, mutilé, nu?

The second line of the couplet is merely a fivefold asyndeton.

5. *La Chambre dorée,* 33-35. Justice flees from France and appeals to God.

> A ce throsne de gloire arriva gemissante
> La Justice fuitive, en sueurs, pantelante,
> Meurtrie & deschiree. . . .

In this case, six terms are accumulated to describe the plight of Justice: she is
"groaning," "fugitive," "sweating," "breathless," "bruised," and "torn."

6. *La Chambre dorée,* 227-232. The corrupt judges.

> Voila en quel estat vivoyent les justiciers,
> Aux meurtriers si benins, des benins les meurtriers,
> Tesmoins du faux tesmoins, les pleiges des faussaires,
> Receleurs des larrons, maquereaux d'adulteres,
> Mercenaires, vendans la langue, la faveur,
> Raison, auctorité, ame, science & cœur.

This passage is particularly rich in baroque stylistic devices. Of such techniques as the echoing of "meurtriers," "benins," and "tesmoins," as well as
the antithetical construction of the second line, more will be said in another
place. At the moment, however, we merely desire to call attention to the seven-
fold heaping of opprobrious epithets upon the judges, followed by the list of
seven things which they are willing to sell.

7. *La Chambre dorée,* 371-373. Description of Cruelty in the form of a Moor.

> Ses levres à gros bords, ses yeux durs de travers,
> Flambans, veineux, tremblans, ses naseaux hauts, ouvers,
> Les sourcils joints, espais, sa voix rude, enrouëe,

One adjective seldom seems to satisfy d'Aubigné: he needs four terms to describe the eyes and two each for the eyebrows and voice.

8. *La Chambre dorée,* 920-926. A contemptuous accumulation of legal
terms, satirizing the procedures of the hated Palais de Justice:

> A plaider, à produire un gros enfantement
> De procez, d'interdits, de griefs; un compulsoire,
> Puis le desrogatoire à un desrogatoire,
> Visa, pareatis, replicque, exceptions,
> Revisions, duplicque, objects, salvations,
> Hypothecques, guever, deguerpir, prealables,
> Fin de non recevoir. . . .

It may perhaps be remarked that Rabelais also, in the *Tiers Livre*, uses a similar technique in accumulating lists of ridiculous legal terms, and indeed that Rabelais' work as a whole abounds in comic or merely exuberant catalogues of picturesque words. This, of course, must be freely admitted; it is not my contention that individual stylistic devices employed by baroque artists are never encountered elsewhere; no single device. taken by itself, ever determines a style.

9. *Les Fers*, 85–87. Satan's speech to God. He lists his actions in eight verbs.

> . . . "Je vien de voir la terre
> La visiter, la ceindre & y faire la guerre,
> Tromper, tenter, ravir, tascher à decevoir
> Le riche en ses plaisirs, le pauvre au desespoir";

10. *Les Fers*, 411–414. Episodes of the Second Religious War. It will be remembered that this was the first in which d'Aubigné participated, so that it presumably produced a particularly strong impression upon his mind.

> Les autres d'autrepart marquent au vif rangees
> Mille troupes en feu, les villes assiegees,
> Les assauts repoussés, & les saccagemens,
> Escarmouches, combats, meurtres, embrazemens.

11. *Les Fers*, 680–684. Cannibalism during the war.

> Ceux-là veulent offrir leurs bergers aux mastins,
> Mais les chiens, respectans le cœur & les entrailles,
> Furent comme chrestiens punis par ces canailles
> Qui, en plusieurs endroits, ont rosti & masché,
> Savouré, avalé, tels cœurs en plain marché:

It is obvious that the poet wishes to dwell upon this eating of human flesh, since he lingers upon the "roasting," "chewing," "savoring," and "swallowing."

12. *Vengeances*, 423–424. Warning to tyrants.

> O tyrans, apprenez, voyez, resolvez vous
> Que rien n'est difficile au celeste courroux;

The second and third verbs are really redundant.

13. *Vengeances*, 478–479. Punishment of Herod.

> Ses cris, son hurlement, son souci, ses adresses
> Ne servirent de rien: . . .

The first line is merely a fourfold asyndeton.

14. *Vengeances*, 485–486. Punishment of another Herod—this one Herod Antipas.

> Souffrit l'exil, la honte, une crainte caïne,
> La pauvreté, la fuite & la fureur divine.

The verb "souffrit" has six direct objects.

15. *Vengeances,* 533–534. The crimes of Nero.

> Mais ton cœur put vouloir, & put ta main meurtriere
> Tuer, brusler, meurtrir precepteur, ville & mere.

This is a curious example, for subject, verb, and direct object are all multiplied.

16. *Vengeances,* 722–724. The persecuted church will be vindicated.

> Cet enfant brisera de ces grands Rois les testes
> Qui l'ont proscript, banni, outragé, dejetté,
> Blessé, chassé, battu de faim, de pauvreté.

Again we have seven verbs in asyndeton, the final one having a double complement.

17. *Vengeances,* 733–740. The true Christian's longing for martyrdom.

> Venez donc pauvreté, faim, fuittes & blessures
> Banissemens, prison, proscriptions, injures;
> Vienne l'heureuse mort, gage pour tout jamais
> De la fin de la guerre & de la douce paix!
> Fuyez, triomphes vains, la richesse & la gloire,
> Plaisirs, prosperité, insolente victoire,
> O pieges dangereux & signes evidens
> Des tenebres, du vers, & grincement de dents!

There are only three verbs in this passage, which otherwise consists largely in a heaping-up of nouns.

18. *Vengeances,* 927–930. Divine retribution.

> Je suis importuné de dire comme Dieu
> Aux Rois, aux ducs, aux chefs, de leur camp au milieu,
> Rendit, exerça, fit, droict, vengeance & merveille,
> Crevant, poussant, frappant, l'œil, l'espaule & l'oreille;

The third and fourth lines are curious; both consist exclusively of three verbs and three direct objects.

19. *Vengeances,* 1113–1116. The Protestant martyrs of Orléans.

> Ceux qui dans Orleans, sans chiens & sans morsures,
> Furent frappés de rage, à qui les mains impures
> Des peres, meres, sœurs & freres, & tuteurs
> Ont apporté la fin, tristes executeurs;

20. *Jugement,* 83–84. Denunciation of religious traitors.

> Vous leur avez vendu, livré, donné en proye
> Ame, sang, vie, honneur: . . .

Three verbs in asyndeton, followed by four direct objects also in asyndeton.

21. *Jugement, 435.* The just man's purpose in life.

> A servir, adorer, contempler, & cognoistre,

22 and 23. *Jugement, 485-486, and 497-498.* Passages adapted from Hermes Trismegistus on the relationship between nature and God.

> Dieu, Nature & pensee, est en soy seulement
> Acte, necessité, fin, renouvellement.
>
> Tout arbre, graine, fleur, & beste tient dequoy
> Se resemer soi-mesme & revivre par soy.

24. *Jugement, 811-822.* Invective against the pope.

> Voici donc, Antechrist, l'extraict des faits et gestes:
> Tes fornications, adulteres, incestes,
> Les pechés où nature est tournee à l'envers,
> La bestialité, les grands bourdeaux ouvers,
> Le tribut exigé, la bulle demandee
> Qui a la sodomie en esté concedée;
> La place de tyran conquise par le fer,
> Les fraudes qu'exerça ce grand tison de l'enfer,
> Les empoisonnemens, assassins, calomnies,
> Les degats des païs, des hommes & des vies
> Pour attraper les clefs; les contrats, les marchés
> Des diables stipulans subtilement couchés;

The foregoing examples, though not exhaustive, are representative of d'Aubigné's technique: to build up lists of words for the sake of achieving weight and emphasis. In many cases the actual sense could be conveyed by a single *mot juste,* but the poet has sought to use every possible verbal resource to hammer home his meaning. In much this way Borromini and other baroque architects added quantities of nonfunctional decoration to their churches in order to increase the impression of size or height. Hence, in the first example, the double use of "menace" and "promet"; in the fourth example, the five different words used to describe the treatment of Coligny; in No. 8, the catalogue of legal terms; in No. 16, the seven verbs expressing the sufferings of the church; in No. 24, the long list of the crimes committed by the pope.

This last example brings us to another aspect of d'Aubigné's "accumulative," "heaping" technique. It is not merely words that the poet delights in piling up; he uses the same method of accumulating scenes and episodes. Much of the power of *Misères* comes from the long catalogue of civil war atrocities;

horror is added to horror for the purpose of overwhelming the reader's emotions. At times, it must be confessed, this method results in artistic failure; even the most convinced admirers of *Les Tragiques* are likely to find the procession of allegorical figures in *La Chambre dorée* labored and tedious. Every conceivable vice, it seems, is present in the law courts and portrayed in much physical detail. Injustice appears on line 237; Avarice on line 249; Ambition, line 261; Envy, line 279; Anger, line 295; Favoritism, line 304; Drunkenness, line 309; Hypocrisy, line 317; Vengeance, line 329; Jealousy, line 333; Inconstancy, line 341; Stupidity, line 346; Ignorance, line 359; Cruelty, line 369; Passion, line 381; Hatred, line 391; Vanity, line 395; Servility, line 418; Clownishness, line 425; Lust, line 433; Weakness, line 439; Sloth, line 443; Immaturity, line 447; Treachery, line 463; Legal Formalism, line 477; Fear, line 505. Clearly the device has its dangers as well as its advantages and d'Aubigné, who has little sense of moderation, does not always know when to stop.

Les Feux is constructed on similar principles: it is little more than a catalogue of martyrdom. The tragic scenes succeed each other like pearls on a necklace. Many of the episodes are vivid and moving but they all have a certain similarity. The poet's desire to honor the heroes of his faith is understandable but partisan spirit has led him into artistic error. The following deaths at the stake are described: James Bainham, line 91; Thomas Cranmer, line 105; Thomas Haux, line 125; Anne Askève, line 147; Lady Jane Grey, line 207; Thomas Bilnee, line 281; William Gardiner, line 291; Agnes Foster, Agnes Snode, and Agnes George, line 324; Florent Venot, line 357; fourteen Protestants of Meaux, line 384; a tennis-ball manufacturer from Avignon, line 391; two brothers from Lyon, line 427; five more martyrs from the same city, line 455; Philippe de Graveron, line 469; Marie d'Adrian, line 527; Anne du Bourg, line 543; Giovanni Mollio di Montalcino, line 619; Nicolas Croquet, Philippe and Richard de Gastines, line 719; an unknown girl mortally wounded at the Massacre of St. Bartholomew, line 997; three Englishmen, line 1103; a capuchin friar who denounced the pope as Antichrist, line 1205; Bernard Palissy, line 1241. The technique is not so seriously abused in *Les Fers;* nevertheless, in addition to the great description of the Massacre of St. Bartholomew which constitutes a large part of this book, we have to read accounts of the massacres which took place in the various provincial cities.

B. The Echo Device

Another stylistic device used by d'Aubigné to attain massiveness and emphasis, although somewhat similar to the techniques just discussed, merits special study. Hatzfeld, in his article "Der Barockstil der religiösen klassischen Lyrik in Frankreich," has pointed out examples of this device, which he calls

Echotechnik, in the shorter religious poems of Corneille and Racine. It con- •
sists essentially in the repetition, after a short interval, of a cardinal word;
sometimes the repetition occurs within the same line, and in any case not later
than in the following line. Typical examples from Corneille are:

> II (Dieu) a pris soin de vous, prenez soin de sa gloire.

and

> Joignons aux voix des saints une sainte harmonie.

Similarly, Racine writes:

> Qui fais changer des temps l'inconstance durée
> Et ne changes jamais. . . .

and

> Fais ton esclave volontaire
> De cet esclave de la mort.[23]

This echo device is one of the salient stylistic features of *Les Tragiques.* It
is of course closely allied to the baroque fondness for verbal conceits and puns,
which we shall examine in another chapter. Aside from its value as poetic
decoration, d'Aubigné undoubtedly feels that it is useful as a means of arresting the reader's attention. The following list, which considerations of space
preclude from being complete, provides some of the more interesting examples.

  1. *Préface,* 289–291.

> Autant de tisons du courroux
> De Dieu courroucé contre nous
> Furent ces troupes blasphemantes:

  2. *Préface,* 368.

> Mon plaisir est de leur desplaire.

Here the echo is modified and becomes an antithesis.

  3. *Préface,* 403–408. D'Aubigné justifies himself for publishing *Les Tragiques.*

> Mon cœur se plaind, l'esprit est las
> De cercher au droit une excuse:
> Je vai le jour me refusant
> Lors que le jour ie te refuse,
> Et ie m'accuse en t'excusant.

Note the echoing of three different words: "excuse," "refuse," and "jour," as
well as the play upon the verbal similarity between "accuse" and "excuse."

23. Examples quoted by Hatzfeld, *op. cit.*

4. *Misères*, 55–58.

Je n'escris plus les feux d'un amour inconu,
Mais, par l'affliction plus sage devenu,
l'entreprens bien plus haut, car j'apprens à ma plume
Un autre feu, auquel la France se consume.

Here the echo-word "feu" is delayed more than usual, as it does not reappear until three lines after its first appearance, but the principle remains the same.

5. *Misères*, 869–871.

Celui qui d'un canon foudroyant extermine
Le rempar ennemi sans brasser sa ruine
Ruine ce qu'il hait, . . .

6. *Misères*, 1193–1194.

Celuy qui meurt pour soi, & en mourant machine
De tuer son tueur, void sa double ruine:

7. *Princes*, 12.

Lisez-le: vous aurez horreur de vostre horreur!

8. *Princes*, 223–224. Denunciation of flatterers.

Vostre sang n'est point sang, vos cœurs ne sont point cœurs,
Mesme il n'y a point d'ame en l'ame des flatteurs,

9. *Princes*, 751.

Si leurs corps sont lepreux, plus lepreuses leurs ames

In this example, the echo is given added force by the contrast between "corps" and "ames"; the love of antithesis is in itself a baroque characteristic, which is studied elsewhere.

10. *La Chambre dorée*, 227–229.

. . . les justiciers,
Aux meurtriers si benins, des benins les meurtriers,
Tesmoins du faux tesmoin, . . .

11. *La Chambre dorée*, 684. Again the evil judges.

Oyans vous n'oyez point, voyans vous n'avez veu

12. *Les Feux*, 154. Martyrdom of Anne Askève.

Contre les durs tourmens elle fut la plus dure;

13. *Les Feux*, 253.

. . . ce geolier, captif de sa captive,

14. *Les Feux*, 369–371. Martyrdom of Venot.

> Mais bruslant il faloit luire à la verité.
> L'homme est un cher flambeau, tel flambeau ne s'alume
> Afin que sous le muys sa lueur se consume.

15. *Les Feux*, 596.

> C'est pour Dieu l'immortel que je meurs en ce point.

16. *Les Feux*, 618.

> Et voir le fin Satan vaincu par la finesse.

These last two examples are variations of the technique, since it is not the actual word which is repeated; a cognate creates the echo.

17. *Les Feux*, 815.

> Serfs de Satan le serf . . .

18. *Les Feux*, 944. Martyrdom of a young boy, Richard de Gastines.

> Aller faire mourir la mort avec ma mort!

19. *Les Feux*, 1252. Comment on the last words of Bernard Palissy.

> . . . La France avoit mestier
> Que ce potier fut Roy, que se Roy fust potier.

20. *Les Fers*, 37. Appearance of Satan before the throne of God.

> Parmi les purs esprits survint l'esprit immonde

In both 19 and 20 contrast heightens the effect of the echo.

21. *Les Fers*, 52–54. God speaks to Satan.

> "D'où viens-tu, faux Satan? que viens-tu faire ici?"
> Lors le trompeur trompé d'asseuré devint blesme,
> L'enchanteur se trouva desenchanté luy-mesme.

22. *Les Fers*, 357–359. The executions after the conspiracy of Amboise.

> . . . luy monstrant le sang fumant & chaud
> Des premiers etestés, puis s'escria tout haut,
> Haussant les mains du sang des siens ensanglantees:

Like No. 18, a double echo, one of the echoes being a cognate word.

23. *Vengeances*, 140.

> Pour changer le grand Dieu qui n'a de changement.

Similar to one of the Racine examples quoted by Hatzfeld.

24. *Vengeances* 192 and 195–196. The guilt of Cain.

Il avoit peur de tout, tout avoit peur de luy:

> . . . les rochers & les bois
> Effrayés abbayoyent au son de ses abois.

25. *Vengeances*, 197–202. Still Cain.

> Sa mort ne peut avoir de mort pour recompense,
> L'enfer n'eut point de morts à punir cette offense,
> Mais autant que de jours il sentit de trespas:
> Vif il ne vescut point, mort il ne mourut pas.
> Il fuit d'effort transi, troublé, tremblant et blesme,
> Il fuit de tout le monde, il s'enfuit de soy-mesme.

26. *Vengeances*, 221–226.

> . . . ô fols à qui il semble
> Qu'en regardant le ciel, le ciel de vous tremble!
> Jadis vos compagnons, compagnons en orgueil
> (Car vous estes moins forts), virent venir à l'œil
> Leur salaire des cieux, les cieux dont les ventailles
> Sans se forcer gaignoyent tant de rudes batailles.

Both of the foregoing examples are of course extraordinarily rich in echoes—especially those depending on "mort" and "fuit" in No. 25, and those depending on "fuit" in No. 26. Each passage also presents a minor echo: "vif," "vescut" in the first, and the repetition of "compagnons" in the second.

27. *Vengeances*, 352–353.

> Lui qui n'avoit esté de meurtres assouvi
> Assouvit les meurtiers, . . .

28. *Vengeances*, 475–477.

> Mais ce cœur sans oreille & ce sein endurci,
> Que l'humaine pitié, que la tendre merci
> N'avoyent sçeu transpercer, fut transpercé d'angoisses;

29. *Vengeances*, 479–480.

> . . . ces indomptés esprits
> Qui n'oyent point crier en vain jettent des cris.

30. *Vengeances*, 530–531. Portrait of Nero.

> Tu ne fus pas Romain envers ta belle Rome;
> D'où l'ame tu receus, l'ame tu fis sortir:

31. *Vengeances*, 771–772. Attack on Thomas Arundel, archbishop of Canterbury. Also *Vengeances*, 775–778.

Ton sein encontre Dieu enflé d'orgueil souffla:
Ta langue blasphemante encontre toy s'enfla,

Tu fermois le passage au subtil vent de Dieu,
Le vent de Dieu passa, le tien n'eut point de lieu.
Au ravisseur de vie en ce poinct fut ravi
Par l'instrument de vivre & l'une & l'autre vie:

32. *Jugement*, 657–658. A scene from the Last Judgment.

Vous les cerchastes lors: ore ils vous cercheront,
Ces corps par vous aimez encor vous aimeront.

33. *Jugement*, 697.

Voici le Fils de l'homme & du grand Dieu le Fils,

34. *Jugement*, 805–808. Appeal to the Holy Ghost for guidance.

. . . que, juge leger,
Je n'attire sur moi jugement pour juger.
Je n'annoncerai donc que ce que tu annonce,
Mais je prononce autant comme ta loy prononce;

One other case of the repetition of a key word is especially remarkable. Indeed the passage in question is so long, and the variations on the basic theme so elaborate, that the term "echo device" is wholly inadequate; however, the stylistic principle is basically the same as in the examples just studied. This is the sermon delivered at the stake by the martyr Giovanni di Montalcino. Over a space of about forty lines the principal Protestant doctrines are expounded; and this is accomplished almost entirely by ringing changes on the word "seul." The true faith, Montalcino proclaims, is summed up in three words— "seul," "seule," and "seulement."

J'ay presché que Jesus nous est *seul* pour hostie,
Seul sacrificateur, qui *seul* se sacrifie:

J'ay dit qu'en la foi *seule* on est justifié,
Et qu'en la *seule* grace est le salut fié:

J'ai presché que le Pape en terre n'est point Dieu
Et qu'il est *seulement* evesque d'un *seul* lieu: [24]

In all, "seul" is used nine times, "seule" four times and "seulement" five times. This eighteenfold repetition is the most extreme example in *Les Tragiques* of d'Aubigné's hammer-blow technique; and while it serves the purpose of emphasis many readers may feel it to be an artistic flaw. As is so often the case, however, it is in its artistic failures that the characteristics of a style may

24. Cf. *Les Feux*, 655–694.

be most readily discerned. There is little doubt that the poet was proud of this tour de force and considered it an added ornament to his poem. For in the baroque age virtuosity was often felt to be a virtue in itself.

C. *Verbs of Violence*

The devices discussed so far aim chiefly at achieving emphasis by sheer accumulation or repetition. Asyndeton, the heaping up of words, the long lists of parallel episodes, the use of the echoing technique—all of these have one thing in common: they add to the impression of massiveness and weight. Emphasis and exaggeration are, however, also attained by another method: the use of verbs suggesting violence. Frequently, to be sure, the very nature of the subject requires such verbs; it would be difficult to describe the scenes of horror of the religious wars, or the slaughter committed on St. Bartholomew's Eve, without energetic and brutal verbs. D'Aubigné's great interest in horror for its own sake is another aspect of the baroque mind which is discussed in the next chapter. But whatever his subject, he prefers to express himself in the most violent manner possible and this task is often entrusted to forcefully picturesque verbs. Thus, to the general impression of mass in *Les Tragiques* is added the factor of movement; and it has long been remarked, in architecture, sculpture, and painting, that the baroque style is characterized by just such a combination of mass and movement.

The poet's predilection for verbs of violence may perhaps best be seen by examining in detail one of the seven books of *Les Tragiques. Misères* is very representative in this respect, although any of the other six sections of the poem would also serve the purpose well; a complete list of examples from the poem as a whole would merely be seven times as long and would be no more instructive.

The very first line contains the verb "s'attaquer"; d'Aubigné's undertaking is one of war and he proposes to attack the Roman legions. He then compares himself to Hannibal, who

Se *fendit* un passage aux Alpes *embrasez*.[25]

The poet, with fiery courage and a bitter heart

Au travers des sept monts *faict breche* au lieu de porte.[26]

He has an unusually brutal image to describe the circumstances surrounding the composition of *Les Tragiques:*

Nous *avortons* ces chants au milieu des armees,[27]

25. *Misères*, 4. In nn. 25–46 the italics are mine.
26. *Misères*, 6.
27. *Misères*, 70.

Even when all due allowance has been made for the sixteenth-century sense of "avorter"—it meant, as Garnier and Plattard have pointed out in their edition, not only to commit abortion but also to give birth under difficult conditions—the expression remains violent. And here it may be observed that d'Aubigné's taste in verbs is connected with his general love of concrete imagery—a question which deserves special attention in another place.

D'Aubigné's Muse, whom he summons not from Hippocrene but from the tomb, howls like a wild animal:

> . . . *bramant* en la sorte
> Que faict la biche apres le fan qu'elle a perdu.[28]

The French kings have been leading lives of feverish crime:

> Adulteres, *souillans* les couches des plus belles
> Des maris *assommez* ou *bannis* pour leur bien,
> Ils *courent sans repos*, . . .[29]

Under the corrupting influence of war, all human ties are forgotten, and crime has become general:

> Le pere *estrangle* au lict le fils, . . .[30]

The criminal no longer makes any attempt to conceal his misdeeds; with impunity the bandit

> . . . estalle son pillage
> Au son de la trompette, . . .[31]

Those in high authority

> . . . vont *sucçans le sang* des nations:[32]

D'Aubigné describes the soul of an innocent murdered child, a civil war victim, ascending to heaven:

> L'ame plaintive alloit en un plus heureux lieu
> *Esclatter sa clameur* au grand throne de Dieu;[33]

He has seen German soldiers devastating France:

> J'ai veu le reistre noir *foudroyer* au travers
> Les masures de France, & comme une tempeste,
> *Emporter* ce qu'il peut, *ravager* tout le reste;[34]

28. *Misères*, 82–83.
29. *Misères*, 202–204.
30. *Misères*, 212.
31. *Misères*, 238–239.
32. *Misères*, 308.
33. *Misères*, 360.
34. *Misères*, 373–375.

The wounded peasant met by the author has only one plea:

> Faictes-moi d'un bon coup & promptement mourir.[35]

At such sights

> Mes cheveux estonnez *herissent* en ma teste;[36]

The following are the words to describe the "scorched-earth policy":

> L'homme, *crevant* de rage & de noire fureur
> Devant les yeux esmeus de ce grand bienfaicteur
> *Foule* aux pieds ses bien-faicts en *villenant* sa grace,
> *Crache* contre le ciel, . . .[37]

Even domestic animals have reverted to savagery:

> Ils *courent* forcenez les personnes vivantes.[38]

Note that the verb "courent" is here transitive and is a technical term drawn from the language of hunting (as in "chasse à courre"). In these tragic times, when the king enters a city, he is trampling upon a dead body:

> Quand son prince la *foulle*, . . .

> Quand le tyran *s'esgaye* en la ville où il entre,
> La ville est un corps mort, il *passe sur son ventre*,[39]

Justice, weeping, has been banished to heaven:

> Au ciel estoit *bannie en pleurant* la justice,[40]

The great diatribe against Catherine de' Medici gives the poet an opportunity to use many verbs of violence. You wish, he charges her, to

> . . . *abbreuver de sang* la soif de ta puissance—[41]

If you had only stayed in Italy,

> Cinq cens mille soldats *n'eussent crevé*, poudreux
> Sur le champ maternel, . . .[42]

However, retribution will soon be at hand:

> . . . l'edifice haut des superbes Lorreins
> Maugré tes estançons *t'accablera* les reins,[43]

35. *Misères*, 392.
36. *Misères*, 429.
37. *Misères*, 443–446.
38. *Misères*, 478.
39. *Misères*, 583–586.
40. *Misères*, 694.
41. *Misères*, 757.
42. *Misères*, 763–764.
43. *Misères*, 807–808.

For France is

> La maison qu'elle *sappe*, & c'est aussi pourquoi
> Elle fait *tresbucher* son ouvrage sur soi.[44]

Catherine carries pestilence wherever she goes; she spends the night howling:

> Elle *infecte* le ciel par la noire fumee
> Qui sort de ses nareaux; . . .
>
> En paisible minuict on *oit ses hurlements*,[45]

Also at night,

> Elle *s'ameute* avec les sorciers . . .
>
> . . . elle *se veautre* aux hideux cimetieres,[46]

D'Aubigné is equally violent about the Cardinal of Lorraine, whom he accuses of incest:

> . . . il a dedans son sang trempé sa paillardise,[47]

And so the catalogue of horrors continues, with all the verbs of energetic action and brutality: "vomissant" (line 1018), "rasez," "pillez," and "embrasez" (lines 1031 and 1032), "trempa dedans le sang" (line 1039), "estrangla les enfans" (line 1040), "chocqué à testes contre testes" (line 1053), "logeoyent en leur sein le poignard" (line 1096), "le corps se tordist par effort" line 1100), "percé premier l'espais d'une bataille" (line 1122), "franchi devant tous la breche par assaut" (line 1124), "se jeter contre espoir dans la ville assiegee" (line 1125), "veautrez l'eschine en bas" (line 1158), "se faisoyent esgorger" (line 1160), "trepigné dans le pré avec bouche embavee" (line 1181), "menace de frayeur & crie en offencant" (line 1183), "Satan grincant les dents" (line 1196), "pippez, pillez, effrayez & battus" (line 1204), "la pantoufle crotter les lys de la couronne" (line 1218), "esgorger" (line 1251), "Toy, Seigneur, qui abbas, qui blesses, qui guéris, Qui donnes vie & mort, qui tue & qui nourris" (lines 1296 and 1297). The closing lines of *Misères* continue the theme of action and energy:

> Ils crachent vers la lune & les voutes celestes:
> N'ont-elles plus de foudre & de feux & de pestes?
> Ne partiront jamais du throsne où tu te sieds
> Et la mort & l'enfer qui dorment à tes pieds?
> Leve ton bras de fer, haste tes pieds de laine,
> Venge ta patience en l'aigreur de la peine,

---

44. *Misères*, 867–868.
45. *Misères*, 890–896, *passim*.
46. *Misères*, 899 and 902.
47. *Misères*, 1002.

Frappe du ciel Babel: les cornes de son front
Desfigurent la terre & lui ostent son rond![48]

Wölfflin has spoken, in his *Renaissance and Baroque,* of the change in *Zeit-geist* which came over western Europe in the latter half of the sixteenth cen-tury, causing men to like to surround themselves with buildings which were imposing in size and at the same time suggested intense movement. This aspect of baroque architecture has also been emphasized by Scott in his *Archi-tecture of Humanism:* the beauty of a church like the Salute in Venice, for example, depends upon the harmonious ordering of mass and apparent move-ment. The stylistic devices of which we have been speaking here would seem to form a parallel to those features of baroque architecture. The "heaping," the "echo," and the verbs of violence which recur so frequently throughout d'Aubigné's poem are of course employed to give added emphasis to the author's meaning; but stylistically they have a life of their own and correspond to the esthetic delight which the baroque spirit found in heavy and agitated things.

In this connection one more device of poetic technique, constantly used throughout *Les Tragiques,* should be mentioned. I refer to the very high pro-portion of run-on lines. Thus *Misères,* consisting of 1380 lines, contains 413 examples of enjambement. *Jugement,* with 1218 lines, has 332 enjambements. In other words, between a third and a quarter of the lines in the poem are run-on. After Malherbe, this practice is proscribed and the alexandrines of suc-ceeding generations produce an impression of self-contained stability and ordered logic. The long series of enjambements in *Les Tragiques* allow mas-sive passages of poetry to be built up without interruption; and since run-on lines must be read with little pause for breath, they also give a sense of head-long speed. Here again *Les Tragiques* presents the typically baroque combina-tion of mass and movement. Whereas the later, classical alexandrine is ideally suited to the clear presentation of well-defined psychological states, the baroque alexandrine is appropriate for the poetry of violence and propaganda.

3. HORROR AND MARTYRDOM

In the baroque age the minds of men were preoccupied with the subject of martyrdom. The schism in Christendom created by the Reformation had made both Catholics and Protestants feel the need of fighting and dying for their faiths. The atmosphere of fanaticism and civil war which pervaded Europe had accustomed men to beholding horror and torture. And so it is that brutal scenes of martyrdom occupy so large a place in the painting of the late sixteenth and seventeenth centuries. Modern taste sometimes finds these pic-

48. *Misères,* 1373-1380.

tures almost unbearable in their horror; however, the twentieth century itself is an age of violence and atrocities and this may help explain the growing favor enjoyed by baroque art. The painting of the Renaissance had, in general, avoided the subject of martyrdom, or had, at least, refrained from too realistic a representation.

In their manner of depicting martyrdom, such painters as Poussin, Domenichino, Ribera, and Rubens reveal the baroque spirit. Readers who are accustomed to thinking of Poussin in terms of classical composition and harmonious repose will be startled by this artist's picture, "Martyrdom of St. Erasmus." [49] The writhing body of the saint, who is grimacing with pain, lies diagonally across the foreground. The central figure, a burly executioner, is pulling the martyr's intestines out with his bare hands; assistants are winding up the intestines on a windlass. A throng of sadistic onlookers press forward so as to miss no detail of the saint's agony. Two cherubs hover in the sky overhead, bearing the martyr's palm and crown, but our attention is not specially drawn to them: the dominant impression is one of physical horror.

In Ribera's "Martyrdom of St. Andrew," indeed, any suggestion of heavenly reward is absent. The artist has been exclusively concerned with the representation of pain. In this respect, as Weisbach points out,[50] the picture is a wholly materialistic one. The saint, who is almost entirely naked, has his outstretched arms tied to a crossbar, which two athletic brutes are hoisting to the top of a pole by means of pulleys. With Spanish realism Ribera makes us see every detail of the texture of the martyr's skin and flesh; above all, the face, with its tortured eyes and mouth, is unbearable in its vividness.

The martyrdom of a woman was felt to be an especially interesting subject, as we can see in Domenichino's "Martyrdom of St. Agnes." [51] Here the executioner has plunged a dagger into St. Agnes' naked breast; the red drops of blood spurt forth, in dramatic contrast to the white skin. The artist has intended, by emphasizing the saint's frailty and femininity, to provide an added fillip of horror. Here again, though the scene is a "two-storeyed" one, with, above, the martyr being welcomed before the throne of God, all our attention is focused on the torture.

A final example, by Rubens, is perhaps the most physically harrowing of all: the "Martyrdom of St. Livinus.[52] The canvass, as is so often the case with this master, is thronged with energetic, whirling figures. The saint, writhing in agony, is kneeling with arms outstretched. One of the executioners, ferociously clenching a knife between his teeth, is eagerly watching the martyr's face for

49. In the Vatican Museum.
50. "The psychological emphasis, in this very materialistic presentation, is placed upon the horror of the event." Weisbach, p. 164. The picture is in the Prado.
51. Bologna, Pinacoteca.
52. Brussels Museum. Reproduced by both Mâle and Weisbach.

signs of pain. Another executioner, with massive forearms, clutches a pair of pliers, which contain St. Livinus' bloody and dripping tongue, and offers this morsel to a large and hungry dog.

D'Aubigné, by his interest in scenes like these, shows himself to be spiritually akin to the great baroque painters. If challenged as to the artistic appropriateness of such subjects he, like Rubens or Ribera, would probably have replied that the vivid representation of scenes of martyrdom served a moral and religious purpose. In an age where religious beliefs were frequently challenged, it was necessary to hold up models of steadfastness and courage; the more gruesome the torture, the greater was the glory of the martyr. Yet, although the baroque artists were motivated by a sincere desire to proclaim the truth of their faith, it is impossible to escape the conclusion that they enjoyed depicting physical horror for its own sake; and all this is certainly the case with d'Aubigné.

There are, in *Les Tragiques,* not only the numerous scenes of Protestant martyrs at the stake; there is also the great picture of the martyrdom of France itself in *Misères.* As a militant Protestant, d'Aubigné is of course seeking to arouse indignation against the enemies of his religion; *Les Tragiques* is a propaganda work, designed to place the blame for the horrors of war on the Catholics. As a poet, however, the author delights in his ability to write forcefully; scenes of horror are especially adapted to his particular genius. And so, despite his sympathy for the French peasants, he tends to dwell, lingeringly and with artistic satisfaction, on their plight, describing the lot of the

> . . . rustic, qui, ayant la journee
> Ta pantelante vie en rechignant gaignee
> Reçois au soir les coups, l'injure & le tourment,
> Et la fuite & la faim, injuste payement.[53]

The tortures inflicted by German soldiers on the innocent peasantry are depicted with the same attention to physical detail that we have seen in baroque painting. The farmers are

> . . . pendus par les doigts
> A des cordons trenchans, ou attachez au bois
> Et couchez dans le feu, ou de graisses flambantes
> Les corps nus tenaillez, ou les plaintes pressantes
> De leurs enfans pendus par les pieds, arrachez
> Du sein qu'ils empoignoyent, des tetins assechez.[54]

In another scene the poet tells us how, wandering through the devastated

53. *Misères,* 257–260.
54. *Misères,* 347–352.

countryside, seeing burning houses, corpses, and hideous faces everywhere, he
heard a dying man crying out for help. Guided by the sound, he saw

> D'un homme demi-mort le chef se debattant,
> Qui sur le sueil d'un huis dissipoit sa cervelle.[55]

The peasant begs d'Aubigné to dispatch him as quickly as possible, and describes how his pregnant wife has been beaten to death. Going inside the
house, the author finds a whimpering child, nearly dead from starvation, and
beside it

> . . . l'horrible anatomie
> De la mere assechee: elle avoit de dehors
> Sur ses reins dissipez trainé, roulé son corps,
> Jambes & bras rompus, une amour maternelle
> L'esmouvant pour autrui beaucoup plus que pour elle.
> A tant ell'approcha sa teste du berceau,
> La releva dessus; il ne sortoit plus d'eau
> De ses yeux consumez; de ses playes mortelles
> Le sang mouilloit l'enfant; point de laict aux mammelles,
> Mais des peaux sans humeur:[56]

This scene, which is very characteristic of one aspect of d'Aubigné's sensibility,
may seem offensive to fastidious modern readers; but the poet's contemporaries
probably would not have questioned its artistic appropriateness. The picture
of the brain oozing out on the doorstep, or of the infant crying beside the
desiccated corpse of the mother belong to the same period of artistic sensibility
as Poussin's St. Erasmus, Rubens' St. Livinus, or of the gouging of Gloucester's
eyes in *King Lear*.

Episodes of cannibalism are not uncommon in *Les Tragiques,* and the poet
generally exploits their possibilities to the full. Perhaps the most horrifying
one occurs in *Misères, 501–562*. A mother, overcome by hunger, seizes a knife
and kills her own child. Then

> De sa levre ternie il sort des feux ardens,
> Elle n'appreste plus les levres, mais les dents,
> Et des baisers changés en rude morsures.
> La faim acheve tout de trois rudes blessures,

Princes likewise presents many scenes of horror. The kings of France,

> Yvres d'ire & de sang, nagent luxurieux
> Sur le sein des putains, . . .[57]

55. *Misères*, 384–385.
56. *Misères*, 414–423.
57. *Princes*, 692–693.

Charles IX shows his sadism in the cruel refinements which he brings to the
sport of hunting:

> . . . sa jeunesse esgaree
> N'aimoit rien que le sang & prenoit sa curee
> A tuer sans pitié les cerfs qui gemissoyent,
> A transpercer les sains & les fans qui naissoyent,[58]

Royal princesses delight in frequenting brothels and abortions are constantly
performed in the Louvre. Again, no detail, however repellent, is spared us:

> Du Louvre les retraits sont hideux cimetieres
> D'enfans vuidez, tuez par les apotiquaires: [59]

This picture, though of questionable taste, is a good sample of d'Aubigné's
technique of emphasizing physical horror by vivid detail. Less physiological,
but also very powerful, is the account of another royal abortion:

> . . . le fol vulgaire conte
> D'un coche qui, courant Paris à la minuict,
> Vole une sage femme, & la bande & conduit
> Prendre, tuer l'enfant d'une Roine masquee,[60]

This night scene, full of violent movement, mystery, and crime, is worthy of
a baroque painter.

The fourth book of the poem, *Les Feux,* which is primarily devoted to the
subject of martyrdom, contains, as might be expected, one gruesome episode
after another. However firm d'Aubigné's belief may be in the spiritual re-
wards awaiting his martyrs in heaven, it is apparent that, as a poet, he is fascinated by the details of their physical suffering—and in this he resembles the
painters we have discussed. In the execution of Thomas Haux, the burning of
the flesh is emphasized:

> Sa face estoit bruslee, & les cordes des bras
> En cendres & charbons estoyent cheutes en bas,
> Quand Haux, en octroyant aux freres leur requeste,
> Des os qui furent bras fit couronne à sa teste.[61]

The martyrdom of Anne Askève provides a subject similar to Domenichino's "Martyrdom of St. Agnes," in that attention can be directed, with
especial emotional effect, to feminine suffering. D'Aubigné emphasizes the
victim's "corps delicat" and describes the executioners' frantic efforts to inflict
pain upon it.

58. *Princes,* 767–770.
59. *Princes,* 1023–1024.
60. *Princes,* 1028–1031.
61. *Les Feux,* 131–134.

Le juge se despite, & luy mesme retend
La corde à double nœud; il met à part sa robe,
L'inquisiteur le suit; la passion desrobe
La pitié de leurs yeux; ils viennent remonter
La gehenne, tourmentez en voulant tourmenter;
Ils dissipent les os, les tendons & les veines,
Mais ils ne touchent point à l'ame par les geines.[62]

This procedure of enumerating the various tortured parts of the body is repeated in the case of Thomas Bilnee, a Cambridge student who was accused of heresy by Thomas More and burned at the stake. D'Aubigné tells us how Bilnee's jailer found the martyr one evening, training himself to bear the pain of fire by holding his finger in the flame of a candle:

Ce feu lent & petit, d'indicible douleur,
A la premiere fois lui affoiblit le cœur,
Mais apres il souffrit brusler à la chandelle
La peau, la chair, les nerfs, les os & la moëlle.[63]

Thomas Gardiner was subjected to a particularly horrible form of torture, of Portuguese origin. He was forced to swallow a towel attached to a string; the executioner then pulled it out forcibly and made him swallow it again:

Il avalla trois fois la serviette sanglante,[64]

Gardiner was then dragged to the stake, had his right hand cut off, was hoisted up on a pulley, and slowly burned. The poet insists on each separate form of torture:

On le traine au supplice, on coupe sa main dextre,
Il la porte à la bouche avec sa main senestre,
La baise; l'autre poing luy est couppé soudain,
Il met la bouche à bas & baise l'autre main.
Alors il est guindé d'une haute poulie,
De cent nœuds à cent fois son ame se deslie,
On brusle ses deux pieds: tant qu'il eut le sentir
On cerche sans trouver en lui le repentir.
La mort à petit feu lui oste son escorce,
Et lui à petit feu oste à la mort la force.[65]

The use of the word "escorce" to describe the slow peeling of the victim's skin as it burns, suggesting the bark of a tree, constitutes a typical image, bearing the unmistakable stamp of d'Aubigné's style.

62. *Les Feux*, 172–178.
63. *Les Feux*, 287–290.
64. *Les Feux*, 305.
65. *Les Feux*, 309–318.

Les Feux is, in effect, like *Misères* and *Les Fers,* a long catalogue of atrocities. In one place the poet describes the "roasted cheeks" of the victim; in another the martyrs, like Rubens' St. Livinus, have their tongues cut out; [66] still elsewhere women are buried alive. We need dwell no further on the details; it is significant to note, however, that d'Aubigné has chosen to celebrate the heroes of his religion, not by giving an account of the deeds they performed, but by insisting minutely on the physical tortures of their martyrdom. In this he parallels the painting of his time; Mâle and Weisbach have shown that the artists of the Counter Reformation generally prefer to depict saints at the moment of suffering and death rather than in action during their lives. This procedure even extends to the representation of the Catholic missionaries to Japan and India, who are shown not carrying out their work but being executed, as in Callot's engraving of the "vingt-trois premiers martyrs mis en croix pour la prédication de la saincte foy au Jappon." [67]

After the book of executions comes the book of massacres. In *Les Fers* we find the same vigorous language, the same lingering over horrible details. When Satan asks God to test the Protestants through prosperity rather than adversity, he urges that they be allowed to taste sadistic pleasures:

> Mets-les à la fumee & au feu des batailles,
> Verse de leurs haineux à leur pieds les entrailles,
> Qu'ils manient du sang; . . .[68]

Though these words are put in the mouth of the devil, their very vividness suggests that d'Aubigné had experienced and enjoyed these sensations during his own career as a soldier.

The fifth book of *Les Tragiques* is a sort of heavenly picture gallery, composed of a series of "tableaux" which d'Aubigné professed to have seen in a vision. The first painting represents a scene which produced a profound impression on the poet as a boy: the conspiracy of Amboise. Bellona, goddess of war, presides over this picture. She

> Ne souffre rien d'entier, veut tout voir à morceaux:
> On la void deschirer de ses ongles ses peaux,
> Ses cheveux gris, sans loy, sont grouillantes viperes
> Qui lui crevent le sein, dos & ventre d'ulceres,
> Tant de coups qu'ils ne font qu'une playe en son corps!
> La louve boit le sang & fait son pain de morts.[69]

This allegorical figure is of course mere decoration; the poet is indulging his fondness for gruesome detail. The actual civil war episode takes place in

66. Cf. *Les Feux*, 496–514.
67. Cf. Mâle, *op. cit.*, p. 118.
68. *Les Fers*, 133–135.
69. *Les Fers*, 329–334.

Amboise itself, and is a reminiscence of the scene he saw when he was eight
years old, passing through the town on his way to Paris with his father:

> . . . une petite ville
> Pleine de corps meurtris en la place estendus,
> Son fleuve de noyés, ses creneaux de pendus.
> Là, dessus l'eschafaut qui tient toute la place,
> Entre les condamnés un esleve sa face
> Vers le ciel, luy monstrant le sang fumant & chaud
> Des premiers etestés, . . .[70]

Another civil war atrocity is the massacre of Vassy: it is the subject of another
"painting." D'Aubigné spends some thirty lines describing how the Duc de
Guise's soldiers set fire to a barn where the Huguenots were holding their
services. As usual, there is an especially horrifying touch: some priests, who
are watching the massacre from a neighboring house, point out the Protestants
who have escaped and make sure that they are dispatched as well. In another
unidentified massacre,

> L'on void dedans le sein de l'enfant transporté
> Le poignard chaud qui sort des poulmons de la mere; [71]

In the Tours massacre,

> . . . on void tirer d'un temple des faux-bourgs
> Trois cens liés, mi-morts, affamés par trois jours,
> Puis delivrés ainsi, quand la bande bouchere
> Les assomma, couplés, au bord de la riviere; [72]

Of course the *tragédie qui efface le reste* is the Massacre of St. Bartholomew;
this constitutes the principal passage in *Les Fers,* extending from line 705 to
line 1190. It seems hardly necessary to quote any more descriptions of atrocities; the important thing to note is that here as elsewhere d'Aubigné pursues
his customary method of increasing the impression of horror by selecting
particularly gruesome details: senators are dragged through the mud, even
small boys are ashamed to be seen without bloodstained hands, princesses flee
in horror from their blood-soaked beds, the beds themselves are described as
"pieges fumans," the Seine has more blood in it than water, a woman hanging
by her hair from a bridge has the stabbed body of her husband thrown on top
of her, the king's mistresses make obscene remarks about the naked corpses
they see lying on the ground, while the king himself, rifle in hand, takes pot-
shots at the Protestants who are too slow to drown in the river.

In a poem dealing with civil war it is not surprising that there should be

70. *Les Fers,* 352–358.
71. *Les Fers,* 580–581.
72. *Les Fers,* 611–614.

many harrowing episodes; the subject itself requires scenes of horror, and from the subject alone it is difficult to arrive at valid conclusions concerning an author's style. But even the choice of a subject implies certain predilections on a writer's part; and it will be apparent to most readers of *Les Tragiques* that d'Aubigné displays a certain *complaisance* in dwelling so repeatedly and so lingeringly on scenes of horror. Furthermore, the poet's unfailing instinct for choosing the brutal, unforgettable detail which will stamp each scene into the memory is indeed a manifestation of style. However, even more significant for the style of d'Aubigné are the numerous violent and repellent metaphors. Here it is no longer a question of reporting historical atrocities; this is the gratuitous use of horror for purposes of poetic embellishment. Perhaps the most famous of these metaphors is the comparison of France to a mother giving suck to two fighting children:

> . . . dessous ta mammelle
> S'esmeut des obstinez la sanglante querelle.[73]

One may criticize the good taste but not the poetic power of this passage:

> Je veux peindre la France une mere affligee
> Qui est entre ses bras de deux enfans chargee.
> Le plus fort, orgueilleux, empoigne les deux bouts
> Des tetins nourriciers; puis, à force de coups
> D'ongles, de poings, de pieds, il brise le partage
> Dont nature donnoit à son besson l'usage; [74]

This metaphor of "un combat dont le champ est la mere" is elaborately developed, occupying thirty-four lines of *Misères;* it culminates in a final outburst of violence:

> Adonc se perd le laict, le suc de sa poitrine;
> Puis, aux derniers abois de sa proche ruine,
> Elle dit: "Vous avez, felons, ensanglanté,
> Le sein qui vous nourrit & qui vous a porté;
> Or vivez de venin, sanglante geniture,
> Je n'ai plus que du sang pour vostre nourriture." [75]

Upon first reading this long metaphor we are likely to be struck primarily by the atmosphere of horror, violence, and blood; a more careful examination, however, will show that the passage is above all intensely physiological. As in the various scenes of martyrdom and massacre which we have been analyzing, the impression of horror derives from the emphasis on physiological detail. A

73. *Misères*, 93–94.
74. *Misères*, 97–102.
75. *Misères*, 125–130.

list of the parts of the body mentioned would include "mammelle," "pis," "tetins," "ongles," "poings," "pieds," "mains," "bras," "yeux," "poitrine," "sein." This preoccupation with the physical is actually an aspect of another element of the baroque style, studied elsewhere: the concreteness of the imagery.

The most physiological of all the metaphors in *Les Tragiques* follows immediately after the comparison of France to the woman nursing two fighting children. In this case, France is likened to a sick giant. D'Aubigné gives us an anatomical analysis calculated to arouse disgust and horror:

> La masse degenere en la melancholie;
> Ce vieil corps tout infect, plein de sa discrasie,
> Hydropique, fait l'eau, si bien que ce geant,
> Qui alloit de ses nerfs ses voisins outrageant,
> Aussi foible que grand n'enfle plus que son ventre.
> Ce ventre dans lequel tout se tire, tout entre,
> Ce faux dispensateur des communs excremens
> N'envoye plus aux bords les justes alimens:
> Des jambes & des bras les os sont sans moelle,
> Il ne va plus en haut pour nourrir la cervelle
> Qu'un chime venimeux dont le cerveau nourri
> Prend matiere et liqueur d'un champignon pourri.[76]

The reader may be tempted to feel that such a passage is more appropriate to a medical textbook than to a religious and patriotic poem; certain aspects of baroque artistic sensibility are indeed difficult for modern taste to admire without reserves. Yet one cannot deny the verbal virtuosity and power of such a passage; and perhaps, after all, a certain literary value should be conceded to shock. The intent to produce shock is, of course, everywhere apparent in *Les Tragiques;* it is allied to the spirit of propaganda which pervades the poem and is indeed an integral part of the baroque style.

One further aspect of d'Aubigné's horror technique should be examined here: the very large part which demonology plays in his poem. A Walpurgis Night atmosphere pervades *Les Tragiques*. This is something more than the purely physical atrocities which we have been considering; at times the very breath of hell seems to blow through these pages. Everywhere we encounter curses, sorcery, demons, and all manner of infernal beings, and this adds another dimension to the feeling of horror so characteristic of the poem. For example, d'Aubigné is not content with accusing Catherine de' Medici of political crimes; in addition, she is charged with devoting her nights to witchcraft:

76. *Misères,* 145–156.

Elle s'ameute avec les sorciers enchanteurs,
Compagne des demons compagnons imposteurs,
Murmurant l'exorcisme et les noires prieres.[77]

She wallows in cemeteries and by incantations lures snakes to dance on the graves. Then she digs up the corpses, breathes satanic spirit into the bones, makes them stand up, covered with earth, and listens to their hoarse voices. In order to manufacture candles for these nocturnal orgies, she slaughters innocent children and melts down their flesh and bones for tallow. The list of ingredients used in her magic brew is reminiscent of the witches' scenes in *Macbeth*:

La teste d'un chat roux, d'un ceraste la peau,
D'un chat-huant le fiel, la langue d'un corbeau,
De la chauve-soris le sang, & de la louve
Le laict chaudement pris sur le point qu'elle trouve
Sa tasniere vollee & son fruict emporté,
Le nombril frais-couppé à l'enfant avorté,
Le cœur d'un vieil crapaut, le foye d'un dipsade,
Les yeux d'un basilic, la dent d'un chien malade,
Et la bave qu'il rend en contemplant les flots,[78]

Although d'Aubigné denounces sorcery as an imposture and denies the reality of the demons conjured up by Catherine, he is betrayed by his poetic imagination. As an austere Protestant, he may profess disbelief in demons; but he is so anxious to prove that Catherine is actually an agent of the infernal powers, and he is himself so fascinated with demonology that witchcraft here assumes the force of reality. Through the poet's creation, in *Les Tragiques* the spirits of hell are frequently endowed with a more vivid life than many of the historical characters. The invisible workings of the devil are felt throughout the poem.

The peasants' houses, during the civil war, are filled with "demons encharnez"; Catherine and the Cardinal of Lorraine have been inflicted on France through an infernal enchantment:

. . . les astres mutinez
Les tirerent d'enfer, puis ils furent donnez
A deux corps vicieux, . . .[79]

The contemporary Frenchman is filled with thoughts of slaughter and when he himself is killed,

77. *Misères*, 899–901.
78. *Misères*, 927–935.
79. *Misères*, 719–721.

Satan grincant les dents le convie aux enfers.[80]

In *Princes* the people do not murmur against the gross corruption of the court because flatterers have taken over the pulpits and have *bewitched* (*ensorcelé*) their congregations; the toleration of sin is thus seen to be the result of satanic witchcraft. Magic operates also in the unjust law courts; one of the allegorical figures appearing in *La Chambre dorée*, Ambition, is compared to the enchantress of *Orlando Furioso*:

C'est une Alcine fausse . . .[81]

Satan himself plays an important part in *Les Fers*. In a scene which is strongly reminiscent of the Book of Job ("And then went Satan forth from the presence of the Lord . . .") the devil obtains from God permission to test the faithful:

Le ciel pur se fendit, se fendant il eslance
Cette peste du ciel aux pestes de la France.
Il trouble tout, passant: car à son devaller
Son precipice esmeut les malices de l'air,
Leur donne pour tambour & chamade un tonnerre;
L'air qui estoit en paix confus se trouve en guerre.
Les esprits des humains, agités de fureurs,
Eurent part au changer des corps superieurs.[82]

Literally as well as figuratively the civil wars are a manifestation of the workings of Satan in the world. Catherine has been possessed by the devil:

Du chef de Jesabel il print possession: [83]

But there have been many other diabolical disguises:

. . . l'enchanteur ruzé
Tantost en conseiller finement desguizé,
En prescheur penitent & en homme d'Eglise,
Il mutine aisément, il conjure, il attise
Le sang, l'esprit, le cœur & l'oreille des grands.[84]

The influence of hell is felt in the Massacre of St. Bartholomew:

Comme si du profond des esveillés enfers
Grouillassent tant de feux, de meurtriers, & de fers,[85]

80. *Misères*, 1196.
81. *La Chambre dorée*, 274.
82. *Les Fers*, 183–190.
83. *Les Fers*, 206.
84. *Les Fers*, 213–217.
85. *Les Fers*, 791–792.

One should not be misled by the "comme si" formula; the poet is not indulging in a mere simile but actually wants us to feel the presence of the infernal powers.

Cardinal Crescentio, who was the legate of the pope at the Council of Trent, is accompanied by a black dog, like Goethe's Faust:

> Crescence, cardinal, qui à ton pourmenoir
> Te vis accompagné du funèbre chien noir,
> Chien qu'on ne put chasser, tu conus ce chien mesme
> Qui t'abayoit au cœur de rage si extreme
> Au concile de Trente: & ce mesme demon
> Dont tu ne sçavois pas la ruze, bien le nom,
> Ce chien te fit prevoir non pourvoir à ta perte.[86]

And in *Jugement* the pope is designated as the eldest son of Satan.[87] In fact, so convinced is d'Aubigné of the workings of the devil in the world that he is at times tempted to think of himself as demoniacally inspired. In one of his numerous hindsight prophecies, or "apophéties," remarkable for its preterition, he says, in effect: "I could, if I chose, foretell all these things, if it did not constitute a wicked use of supernatural powers."

> "Encore, pour l'advenir, te puis-je faire voir
> Par l'aide des demons, au magicien miroir,
> Tels loyers reçeus; mais ta tendre conscience
> Te fait jetter au loing cette brave science:" [88]

Despite this disclaimer, however, the demoniacal spirit is allowed to operate and various dire events are prophesied.

In recapitulation, it may be said that just as horror and martyrdom occupy a large place in baroque painting, so also they are a favorite subject with d'Aubigné in *Les Tragiques*. Like Rubens and Ribera and Domenichino, d'Aubigné tends to stress the physiological details of suffering. But this interest in horror transcends any mere question of subject matter; that it constitutes a definite type of human sensibility, a particular stylistic manner, is shown by the poet's fondness for horrifying metaphors. Finally, despite all his close attention to the physical, d'Aubigné does not confine himself to material horror but conjures up demons as well.

86. *Vengeances*, 1011–1017.
87. *Jugement*, 825.
88. *Princes*, 1241–1244.

Chapter II: SPECTACLE

1. THEATRICALITY

BAROQUE art is characterized by dramatic display. There can be observed, in the painting, sculpture, and architecture of the late sixteenth and seventeenth centuries a constant striving for magnificence and theatrical effects. Such a picture as Rubens' "Miracles of St. Ignatius Loyola" [1] is representative of this tendency. As we look upon this scene of the saint healing the possessed, we have almost the impression of witnessing the finale of an opera. St. Ignatius, his right arm extended in a gesture of benediction, stands majestically at the top of the altar steps, with the huge marble columns of a magnificent nave receding into the distance. A vast throng is present: some are gazing in awe at the saint, while others try to restrain the writhing madmen. Meanwhile, cherubim descend from heaven and hover above St. Ignatius' head. This mixture of drama and pageantry is to be found everywhere in the work of Rubens; among his purely secular paintings the famous series celebrating the marriage of Henri IV and Marie de Médicis, in the Louvre, is especially noteworthy for its pomp and theatrical splendor. Even compositions involving relatively few figures, such as his "Descent from the Cross," [2] appear as if spotlighted for dramatic effect. Sometimes, as in the Medici series, the pageantry is primarily on a human level; at other times, as in the St. Ignatius or St. Francis [3] pictures, the spectacular scenes are on two levels, earthly and heavenly; finally, there are paintings like the "Last Judgment" [4] where a supernatural drama is being enacted.

The student who surveys the field of baroque art will find these three types of theatrical scenes: the purely human or historical, the purely supernatural, and a mingling of the two. It is perhaps the mingling which is most typically baroque. These two-level operatic tableaux may be most strikingly observed in the paintings of El Greco. Two of this artist's works in the Chapter Hall of the Escorial—the "Dream of Philip II" and the "Martyrdom of St. Maurice and the Theban Legion"—are excellent examples of the spectacular mingling of human and supernatural drama. However, El Greco's masterpiece, the "Burial

1. Vienna Museum.
2. Antwerp Museum.
3. "The Communion of St. Francis," Antwerp Museum.
4. Munich, Alte Pinakothek.

of Count Orgaz," [5] which is likely to be most present to the reader's mind, illustrates the same principle. The lower half of this picture is a scene of solemn ceremony, noteworthy for its splendid array of historical portraits; save for the miraculous attendance of SS. Stephen and Augustine with the body of Count Orgaz, the pageantry is human and realistic. But in the upper half, enthroned upon clouds, are Christ, the Virgin Mary, and the nobles of the kingdom of heaven.

Such examples of theatrical art, with the human and divine elements present in varying degrees, could be multiplied almost indefinitely. Suffice it to call attention, in passing, to the magnificent ceiling paintings of the Roman baroque—as, for instance, Cortona's "Miracle of St. Philip Neri," [6] or Pozzi's "Glorification of the Company of Jesus." [7] The greatest works of the leading baroque sculptor, Bernini, are theatrical in effect and present a mingling of human and supernatural elements. In the monument for Pope Urban VIII [8] a skeleton waves an hourglass at the kneeling figure of the pontiff. In the Cattedra Petri, above the throne of St. Peter, the Holy Ghost appears in a burst of glory, surrounded by an operatic array of heavenly figures. But Bernini's most striking work is undoubtedly the "Vision of Santa Teresa"; [9] and here the naturally theatrical effect of the scene is enhanced in two significant ways. First of all, the saint and the angel have been given an architectural·frame which looks like a stage; then,'across the aisle, a group of cardinals has been represented as if sitting in a box at the theater, witnessing a performance. It is as if the artist, proud of his tour de force and confident of the emotion he has aroused in the beholder, were saying: "You believed this to be real—but it's only a theatrical performance. I am so sure of my skill that I know you will continue to be moved even after I have shown you that it is all an illusion!"

Similar in effect are the outstanding architectural achievements of the baroque age. The façades of the great Roman churches—Borromini's Sant'-Agnese, Vignola's Gesù, Maderna's St. Peter's—are above all magnificent and spectacular. The interiors create the impression of being splendid settings for an opera. Sometimes, as in the case of Bernini's Sant'Andrea al Quirinale or Rainaldi's Santa Maria in Campitelli, all the illusionistic tricks of the architect's skill have been called upon to make a small space appear a vast and dramatic one. [10] The great public squares of Rome, in which several buildings, fountains, or other architectural features are combined to form a picturesque unity, likewise strike the observer as theatrical. The Piazza del Popolo and

5. In the Church of St. Thomas, Toledo.
6. Santa Maria in Vallicella, Rome.
7. In the Church of San Ignazio, Rome.
8. St. Peter's, Rome.
9. Santa Maria della Vittoria, Rome.
10. See Fokker or Magni for photographs.

especially the Piazza San Pietro seem to be designed primarily as settings for spectacular pageants in which worldly and religious elements are blended.
As we read *Les Tragiques* we come to realize that here too we are in the presence of spectacle. We shall find, also, that this "theatrical" poetry combines, in varying proportions, the same elements of human and divine pageantry which we have recognized in baroque painting, sculpture, and architecture. It will be convenient, however, to begin by considering the scenes of purely human theatricality.

The very opening lines of *Misères* contain metaphors which are theatrical in character and suggestive of large-scale historical scenes. For example, the author compares his militantly Protestant campaign to the crossing of the Alps by Hannibal:

> Puisqu'il faut s'attaquer aux legions de Rome,
> Aux monstres d'Italie, il faudra faire comme
> Hannibal, qui par feux d'aigre humeur arrosez
> Se fendit un passage aux Alpes embrasez.[11]

A few lines further on, d'Aubigné compares himself to Caesar:

> Il vid Rome tremblante, affreuze, eschevelee,
> Qui en pleurs, en sanglots, mi-morte, desolee,
> Tordant ses doigts, fermoit, defendoit de ses mains
> A Cezar le chemin au sang de ses germains.[12]

The poet's fondness for visual imagery is a question which deserves special study in another place; however, in the passages just quoted, there is more than concreteness of expression, more than an appeal to the eyes. We seem to be looking at vast historical scenes, crowded with agitated figures, where spectacular dramas are being enacted.

The two parallel passages, one describing a good old king and the other an evil modern tyrant as each pays an official visit to a provincial city, are fine examples of pageantry in poetry:

> Jadis nos Rois anciens, vrais peres & vrais Rois,
> Nourrissons de la France, en faisant quelquesfois
> Le tour de leur païs en diverses contrees,
> Faisoyent par les citez de superbes entrees.
> Chacun s'esjouissoit, on sçavoit bien pourquoy;
> Les enfans de quatre ans crioyent: vive le Roy!

On the other hand,

> Nos tyrans aujourd'hui entrent d'une autre sorte,
> La ville qui les void a visage de morte.

11. *Misères*, 1–4.
12. *Misères*, 9–12.

> Quand son prince la foulle, il la void de tels yeux
> Que Neron voyoit Romm' en l'esclat de ses feux;
> Quand le tyran s'esgaye en la ville où il entre,
> La ville est un corps mort, il passe sur son ventre,[13]

The existence of drama implies an audience, and in both cases the poet has pointed to spectators of the scene (the children crying "vive le Roy" and the "visage de morte"). It is characteristic of the art of the late sixteenth and seventeenth centuries to delight in representing thronged scenes of royal ceremony; and these two royal entries call to mind, for example, some of the great historical canvasses of Rubens.

D'Aubigné feels strongly the dramatic effectiveness of depicting large crowds who witness a fateful event. When, in *Misères*, the growth of Catherine de' Medici's political influence is likened to the appearance in the heavens of a sinister comet, the poet develops this metaphor into a crowded dramatic tableau:

> . . . sa force secrette
> Espouvante chacun du regard d'un comette.
> Le peuple, à gros amas aux places ameuté,
> Bee douteusement sur la calamité,
> Et dit: "Ce feu menace & promet à la terre,
> Louche, pasle ou flambant, peste, famine ou guerre."[14]

In this thronged scene, an element of supernatural significance is added to the human drama.

Certain lines in the prayer at the end of *Misères* almost suggest a scene from an opera:

> "Quoi! serons-nous muets, serons-nous sans oreilles?
> Sans mouvoir, sans chanter, sans ouïr tes merveilles?
> As-tu esteint en nous ton sanctuaire? Non,
> De nos temples vivans sortira ton renom."[15]

The poet is always aware of the dramatic character of the events which are afflicting France. In the beginning of *Princes*, defending himself against the charge of accumulating horror upon horror in his poem, he explains that in reality he would like to call a halt to the terrible tragedy which he is witnessing but that moral duty obliges him to expose the criminals who are ruining France. Despite his attempts to justify himself for including so many gruesome episodes in *Les Tragiques*, one is tempted to believe that he enjoys just such scenes for their dramatic possibilities:

13. *Misères*, 563–568 and 581–586.
14. *Misères*, 709–714.
15. *Misères*, 1337–1340.

> Non, il n'est plus permis sa veine desguiser,
> La main peut s'endormir, non l'ame reposer,
> Et voir en mesme temps nostre mere hardie
> Sur ses costez jouër si dure tragedie,
> Proche à sa catastrophe, où tant d'actes passez
> Me font frapper des mains & dire: c'est assez.[16]

The protestations are not altogether convincing. The use of the word "tragedie" is certainly significant; and while "actes" and "catastrophe" are susceptible of a literal and historical interpretation, they have theatrical overtones and reveal the poet's taste for the tragic and spectacular. In this connection the very title of the work as a whole is suggestive. It has often been pointed out that this extraordinary poem contains many elements besides the purely tragic (among others, satire and religious propaganda); but the name *Les Tragiques* reveals what the author has chosen to stress. As he says elsewhere in *Princes,*

> . . . ce siecle n'est rien qu'une histoire tragique,[17]

The misdeeds of the royal family frequently lend themselves to a theatrical presentation. Queen Marguerite's clandestine accouchement, for example, is described in the following manner:

> Je sens les froids tressauts de frayeur et de honte,
> Quand, sans crainte, tout haut, le fol vulgaire conte
> D'un coche qui, courant Paris à la minuict,
> Vole une sage femme, & la bande & conduit
> Prendre, tuer l'enfant d'une Roine masquee,[18]

In a few lines, the poet has succeeded in creating an extraordinarily vivid scene. It is significant to note that we have both a drama and spectators: not only the kidnaped midwife, the midnight coach, and the masked queen, but also the amazed populace watching and commenting upon the scene. This procedure, which presents analogies to Bernini's frank avowal of his "Santa Teresa" as pure theater, is not infrequent in *Les Tragiques.* D'Aubigné, after creating a theatrical picture, often likes to turn his attention to spectators and thereby betrays his awareness and enjoyment of drama: the successful producer is pointing out, with complacent satisfaction, the enthrallment of his audience.

The picture of Henri III, cowering in mortal fear of divine retribution for his sexual misdemeanors, is likewise vivid and melodramatic:

> Quand j'oy qu'un Roy transi, effrayé du tonnerre,
> Se couvre d'une voute & se cache sous terre,

16. *Princes,* 79–84.
17. *Princes,* 206.
18. *Princes,* 1027–1031.

S'embusque de lauriers, fait les cloches sonner,
Son peché poursuivi poursuit de l'estonner,[19]

There are, of course, other aspects of this passage—the violence of moral indignation and the effective use of visual imagery—which present baroque traits. It is frequently possible, as in this case, to consider a single passage baroque in a number of different ways; but here we are concerned with the spectacular and dramatic aspects of the picture.

Similarly, the episode of the virtuous youth who visits the Valois court, interesting as an example of d'Aubigné's handling of allegory, is also noteworthy for its dramatic presentation. The story occupies some four hundred lines at the close of *Princes* and its theatrical possibilities are fully exploited. The poet begins by describing a virtuous old father who has devoted his life to the education of his son. We see the innocent young man arrive at court, where he is at first dazzled by the magnificence and then disgusted by the atmosphere of sycophancy. While he is standing withdrawn from the crowd, lost in his own thoughts, he notices certain men who are surrounded by an adoring throng of army officers and noblemen. He concludes that these men must in some way have distinguished themselves in the service of France but discovers, to his amazement, that they are just the "mignons" of the king. The revelation comes to him with dramatic surprise; disillusioned, he retires to his room. There, suddenly, at midnight, Fortune appears, wearing a coat of mail and leading two naked blindfolded children. She makes a long speech of some two hundred lines, full of cynical advice as to the best practical means of succeeding at court. Her insinuating blandishments are suddenly interrupted by the abrupt arrival in the bedroom of Virtue. Fortune and the two children immediately turn into demons, then into smoke, and finally vanish altogether. This episode of moral allegory, which might have been extremely boring, is rescued from dullness by two baroque techniques: dramatic presentation and great vividness of visual imagery. (For a discussion of the latter of these two aspects, see Chapter III, 2: Personification.)

The Spanish Inquisition naturally arouses d'Aubigné's anger, but even in the midst of indignation he is not unappreciative of the theatrical aspects of public torture. The militant Protestant does not submerge the artist who loves dramatic effects. And so, in *La Chambre dorée*, we have an important passage which dwells upon the auto-da-fé as a public spectacle:

L'Europe se monstra: Dieu vid sa contenance
Fumeuse par les feux esmeus sur l'innocence,
Vid les publiques lieux, les palais les plus beaux
Pleins de peuples bruyans, qui pour les jeux nouveaux

19. *Princes*, 1043–1046.

Estaloyent à la mort les plus entieres vies
En spectacles plaisans & feintes tragedies.
Là le peuple amassé n'amolissoit son cœur,
L'esprit, preoccupé de faux zele d'erreur,
D'injures & de cris estouffoit la priere
Et les plaints des mourans; là, de mesme maniere
Qu'aux theatres on vid s'eschauffer les Romains,
Ce peuple desbauché applaudissoit des mains.[20]

The use of the words "spectacles," "tragedies," "theatres," and "applaudissoit" is significant. This is another great canvass, filled with tragic events and thronged with multitudes of people. Not only is the scene spectacular in itself but d'Aubigné has further emphasized its theatrical character by insisting so much on the reactions of the spectators. This is the double theatricality which we have repeatedly noted: not content with creating a theatrical scene the poet turns aside and points out the audience which is witnessing the drama.

Even when historical events are alluded to in passing they frequently impress us as vivid scenes from a play. Such, for example, is the case with the judgment of Solomon, which is mentioned along with many other episodes of biblical justice, in *La Chambre dorée*. The incident is truly remarkable for compression and dramatic effect:

Là sont peintes les mains qui font mesme serment,
L'une juste dit vrai, l'autre perfidement.
On void l'enfant en l'air par deux soldats suspendre,
L'affamé coutelas qui brille pour le fendre,
Des deux meres le front, l'un pasle & sans pitié,
L'autre la larme à l'oeil, toute en feu d'amitié.[21]

The expressions "là sont peintes" and "on void" reveal that the scene is consciously thought of as a dramatic picture; as in previous examples the poet calls attention to possible spectators and the general theatrical aspect is thereby emphasized. It should be borne in mind, also, that this episode is not essential to the main action of *Les Tragiques;* the writer who gives such dramatic power to a purely parenthetical episode has indeed the instincts of a playwright or a director.

The book of the martyrs, *Les Feux*, contains many spectacular scenes. It opens with a great picture of pageantry, suggestive, like so much else in *Les Tragiques,* of Rubens or Tintoretto or El Greco:

Voici marcher de rang par la porte doree,
L'enseigne d'Israel dans le ciel arboree,

20. *La Chambre dorée*, 613–624.
21. *La Chambre dorée*, 723–728.

> Les vainqueurs de Sion, qui au prix de leur sang
> Portans l'escharpe blanche ont pris le caillou blanc:
> Ouvre, Jerusalem, tes magnifiques portes;
> Le lion de Juda suivi de ses cohortes
> Veut regner, triompher & planter dedans toy
> L'estendart glorieux, l'auriflam de la foy.[22]

When, in the painting of the period 1550–1700, we find this mixture of vivid color, magnificence, and pageantry we recognize at once the baroque style; and therefore it seems appropriate to give the same name to poetry exhibiting these characteristics. *Les Feux* contains too many pictures of this kind for detailed enumeration here; some of them, moreover, have been discussed in Chapter I, 3: Horror and Martyrdom; a few more, however, should be mentioned. One of the martyrs is a maker of tennis balls who lived in Avignon; he attracts d'Aubigné's favorable attention for having publicly denounced the carrying of the Host through the streets. The story gives the poet an opportunity to describe a solemn religious procession witnessed by large crowds:

> Mais surtout on oyoit ses exhortations
> Quand l'idole passoit en ses processions
> Sous les pieds de son throne, & le peuple prophane
> Trembloit à cette voix plus qu'à la tramontane.[23]

In the prolonged martyrology of this book, one theatrical death follows another in rapid sequence. The death of two Protestant brothers at Lyon is typical of many such scenes. The example is offered here at some length as it gives an idea of d'Aubigné's technique of describing executions:

> Ces deux freres prioyent quand, pour rompre leur voix,
> Le peuple forcenant porta le feu au bois:
> Le feu leger s'enleve & bruyant se courrouce,
> Quand contre luy un vent s'esleve & le repousse,
> Mettant ce mont, du feu & sa rage, à l'escart:
> Les freres achevans leurs prieres à part
> Demeurent sans ardeur. La priere finie,
> Le vulgaire animé entreprend sur leur vie,
> Perce de mille coups des fideles les corps,
> Les couvre de fagots: ceux qu'on tenoit pour morts,
> Quand le feu eut bruslé leurs cables, se leverent,
> Et leurs poulmons bruslans, pleins de feu, s'escrierent
> Par plusieurs fois: *Christ, Christ!* & ce mot, bien sonné
> Dans les costes sans chair, fit le peuple estonné:

22. *Les Feux*, 1–8.
23. *Les Feux*, 411–414.

> Contre ces faits de Dieu, dont les spectateurs vivent,
> Estonnez, non changez, leurs fureurs ils poursuivent.[24]

This might be the closing scene of a very sensational opera; and here again, as if to make sure that the reader appreciates its spectacular quality, the poet, in the next to last line, mentions the "spectateurs." For other spectacular martyrdoms the reader is referred to the account of the death of Giovanni di Montalcino (*Les Feux*, 619–710), whose final cry is an exultant

> Vive Christ, vive Christ! & meure Montalchine!

and to the story of Nicolas Croquet, Philippe and Richard de Gastines (*Les Feux*, 719–980). The first two of these Protestant martyrs were, respectively, the uncle and father of the third, who was a mere child at the time that they were all put to death. Despite an ardent faith and a great courage, the boy was overcome by emotion when he saw

> L'honnorable regard & la vieillesse grise
> De son pere & son oncle à un posteau liés.

The father, weeping at his son's show of weakness, reproved him:

> "C'est donc en pleurs amers que j'iray au tombeau,
> Mon fils, mon cher espoir, mais plus cruel bourreau
> De ton pere affligé: car la mort pasle et blesme
> Ne brise point mon cœur comme tu fais toy mesme."

The child, regaining at once his faith and courage, exclaimed

> "Mourons, peres, mourons!"

and all three died a heroic death. In commenting on this dramatic story d'Aubigné remarks that the happiest martyrs are those who perish "au milieu des spectateurs esleus"; thus an audience is highly desirable:

> Mais les martyrs ont eu moins de contentement
> De qui la laide nuict cache le beau tourment: [25]

Theatricality is not only an artistic virtue but a religious one as well. We have seen that, as a poet, d'Aubigné has a predilection for the dramatic and spectacular; now we observe that, even in the realm of religious feeling, he exalts them. It has often been remarked that baroque art prefers to express religious emotions in a theatrical manner. This trait of d'Aubigné's sensibility makes him akin to Bernini and is, I feel, a further way in which the Huguenot poet may be regarded as baroque.

24. *Les Feux*, 439–454.
25. *Les Feux*, 987–988.

In *Les Fers* d'Aubigné has employed a very curious device to tell the story of the religious wars. He has imagined a series of vast pictures painted by the angels in heaven for the contemplation of the elect. In these pictures Coligny and the other Protestant heroes can see represented important events of recent French history. By the very nature of their subject matter, therefore, these canvasses are reminiscent of historical and battle scenes by Rubens. Typical subjects are the *conjuration d'Amboise*, the Protestant siege of Paris in 1567, and the Massacre of St. Bartholomew. The last of these gives d'Aubigné ample opportunity to give vent to his love of the theatrical and forms one of the most spectacular sections in all *Les Tragiques*. For a full appreciation of the sensational and gory details the reader should consult *Les Fers*, lines 705–1190. In this place, I wish to call attention to just one passage, which clearly shows that d'Aubigné conceived of the massacre in terms of drama. After several hundred lines describing wholesale slaughter the scene shifts to the windows of the Louvre, where the king and his mistresses are watching the spectacle. To be sure, one aspect of the passage is that it arouses the indignation of the reader against the rulers of France; d'Aubigné's purpose is, in part, political and religious propaganda. However, in another way, there is an essentially artistic reason for the episode. As in a number of previous instances the poet seems to be saying: "You have been fascinated by the scenes of horror which I have laid before your eyes. But, you see, what I have been doing is to write a play. Now here are the spectators of my tragedy!" In other words, this is self-conscious theatricality.

> Or, cependant qu'ainsi par la ville on travaille,
> Le Louvre retentit, devient champ de bataille,
> Sert après d'eschafaut, quand fenestres, creneaux
> Et terrasses servoyent à contempler les eaux
> Si encores sont eaux. Les dames mi-coiffees
> A plaire à leurs mignons s'essayent eschauffees,
> Remarquent les meurtris, les membres, les beautés,
> Bouffonnent salement sur leurs infirmités.
> A l'heure que le ciel fume de sang & d'ames,
> Elles ne plaignent rien que les cheveux des dames.
> C'est à qui aura lieu à marquer de plus prés
> Celles que l'on esgorge & que l'on jette aprés,
> Les unes qu'ils forçoyent avec mortelles pointes
> D'elles mesmes tomber, pensant avoir esteintes
> Les ames quand & quand, que Dieu ne pouvant voir
> Le martyre forcé prendroit pour desespoir
> Le cœur bien esperant. Nostre Sardanapale
> Ridé, hideux, changeant, tantost feu, tantost pasle
> Spectateur, par ses cris tous enroüés servoit

De trompette aux maraux; le hasardeux avoit
Armé son lasche corps; sa valeur estonnee
Fut, au lieu de conseil, de putains entournee;
Ce Roy, non juste Roy, mais juste harquebusier,
Giboyoit aux passans trop tardifs à noyer! [26]

In the end the spectators become actors in the drama themselves. It would
be difficult to find a more theatrical passage than this one: a vast battle raging
in the streets of Paris, hundreds of Protestants being slaughtered, bleeding
corpses being thrown into the Seine, the king of France sniping at escaping
victims. But the dramatic quality of the scene is thrown into striking relief
by the presence of spectators. Despite all his militant Protestantism, d'Aubigné
remains a conscious artist interested in tragedy. By taking us to the balconies
of the Louvre, where the king's mistresses, in décolleté, are making obscene
remarks, he withdraws us from the thick of the melee just enough to give
us perspective and to make us appreciate the Massacre of St. Bartholomew as
drama.

2. THE *Merveilleux chrétien*

De la foi d'un chrétien les mystères terribles
D'ornements égayés ne sont point susceptibles: [27]

In issuing this directive Boileau undoubtedly had Desmarets de Saint-Sorlin
rather than Agrippa d'Aubigné in mind. The author of *Clovis* and of *Marie-
Madeleine* had, only two years before the publication of *L'Art poétique,* referred to Boileau as an "homme sans foi," and had composed a "Discours pour
prouver que les sujets chrétiens sont les seuls propres à la poésie héroïque." [28]
Had d'Aubigné been alive at the time he would very probably have agreed
with Desmarets; but, in any event, Boileau carried the day and after 1674 the
Christian epic was never again attempted in France.

Though Boileau does not deign to mention d'Aubigné in *L'Art poétique,*
one can feel certain that he disapproved of *Les Tragiques.* There are, throughout this Christian epic, many scenes which combine human and supernatural
events. On one plane, realistically described, we have the actions of history;
but just above, on another plane, are hovering God and His angels. Two paintings by El Greco which present an interesting combination of the realistic and
the supernatural—the "Martyrdom of St. Maurice" and the "Burial of Count
Orgaz"—have already been discussed. We can find, in d'Aubigné's poem,
many counterparts of this baroque technique. Many of his most spectacular

---

26. *Les Fers,* 929–952.
27. *L'Art poétique,* III, 199–200.
28. Cf. Boileau, Clarac edition, p. 233.

scenes are theatrical on two levels: that of human pageantry and history and that of heavenly glory. In such pictures there is suggested a kind of mutual interaction between heaven and earth; and so, following the example of Hatzfeld, it seems appropriate to term this the Jacob's ladder motif.[29] From the very first pages of *Les Tragiques* we find a close involvement of heaven in human events, a constant contact between God and man. This is not invariably expressed in spectacular terms, although we shall find that the most memorable of the passages employing this *merveilleux chrétien* are indeed highly theatrical. The examination of a few specific passages should lead us to a more precise understanding of this Jacob's ladder motif.

In the opening invocation of *Misères,* d'Aubigné calls for divine guidance in his literary task:

> Pour Mercures croisez, au lieu de Pyramides,
> J'ai de jour le pilier, de nuict les feux pour guides.
> Astres secourez-moi: . . .[30]

Strictly speaking, this is a metaphor drawn from the flight of the Israelites from Egypt,[31] and yet d'Aubigné's religious faith makes the image a very powerful and real one; to this man, God is ever-present, watching over human affairs and taking part in the drama of history. It is with a genuine hope of actual divine intervention that, amid the miseries of sixteenth-century France, the Protestant cries out for aid against the hardhearted:

> Tout-Puissant, tout-voyant, qui du haut des hauts cieux
> Fends les cœurs plus serrez par l'esclair de tes yeux,[32]

Heaven is waiting to receive the innocent children who die of starvation during the civil wars:

> L'ame plaintive alloit en un plus heureux lieu
> Esclatter sa clameur au grand throne de Dieu;[33]

When the poet turns to speak of the early Christian martyrs, he immediately envisions an El Greco-like picture:

> Le premier champion de la haute querelle
> Prioit pour ses meurtriers & voyoit en priant
> Sa place au ciel ouvert, son Christ l'y conviant.
> Celuy qui meurt pour soi, & en mourant machine

29. Hatzfeld, "Der Barockstil der religiösen klassischen Lyrik in Frankreich."
30. *Misères,* 21–23.
31. Cf. Exodus 13 and 14.
32. *Misères,* 35–36.
33. *Misères,* 359–360.

De tuer son tueur, voit sa double ruine:
Il void sa place preste aux abysmes ouverts,
Satan grinçant les dents le convie aux enfers.[34]

The ruthless murderer of d'Aubigné's day is thus contrasted with St. Stephen and his vision of hell is no less real than the first martyr's vision of heaven. The world of the *merveilleux chrétien* exists as much in the late sixteenth century as it did for the early Christians. The great prayer which closes the book of *Misères* expresses the feeling that heaven and hell are very close to this world. Particularly worthy of study, however, are some of the more spectacular scenes, where a drama is being enacted simultaneously on earth and in heaven.

La Chambre dorée, though primarily devoted to the problem of legal corruption, opens with a magnificent picture of God and the angels in heaven:

Au palais flamboyant du haut ciel empyree
Reluit l'Eternité en presence adoree
Par les Anges heureux: trois fois trois rangs de vens,
Puissance du haut ciel, y assistent servans.
Les sainctes legions sur leurs pieds toutes prestes
Levent aux pieds de Dieu leurs precieuses testes
Sous un clair pavillon d'un grand arc de couleurs.
Au moindre clin de l'œil du Seigneur des Seigneurs
Ils partent de la main: ce troupeau sacré vole
Comme vent descoché au vent de la parole,
Soit pour estre des Saincts les bergers curieux,
Les preserver de mal, se camper autour d'eux,
Leur servir de flambeau en la nuict plus obscure,
Les defendre d'injure, & destourner l'injure
Sur le chef des tyrans; soit pour d'un bras armé
Desployer du grand Dieu le courroux animé.[35]

This passage bears the characteristic stamp of d'Aubigné's style. All readers will undoubtedly agree that it is remarkable for magnificence and visual splendor: gleaming light, throngs of angels, rainbow of color. But beyond this it is important to note that God's intervention in human affairs is everywhere affirmed: from heaven, the angels descend on earth to protect saints in the night and to fight among the legions of the faithful. It is this interaction between heaven and earth that merits the name of Jacob's ladder motif. While the theatrical scene here is laid primarily in heaven, the presence, on another plane, of the earth, is continually suggested.

34. *Misères,* 1190–1196.
35. *La Chambre dorée,* 1–16.

The motif appears again when the hosts of Protestant martyrs arrive in heaven from their places of torture on earth; the poet describes their tragic and glorious procession:

> Là les bandes du ciel, humbles, agenouillees
> Presenterent à Dieu mil ames despouillees
> De leur corps par les feux, les cordes, les couteaux,
> Qui, libres au sortir des ongles des bourreaux,
> Toutes blanches au feu volent avec les flammes,
> Pures dans les cieux purs, le beau pays des ames,
> Passent l'ether, le feu, percent le beau des cieux.
> Les orbes tournoyans sonnent harmonieux:
> A eux se joinct la voix des Anges de lumiere,
> Qui menent ces presens en leur place premiere.[36]

Such a scene, with the blessed ascending to heaven, the singing angels and the music of the spheres, is one that few artists have attempted. With the Jacob's ladder motif linking the earthly and heavenly levels, it is suggestive of the painting of Murillo, Tintoretto, or El Greco, and yet with the presence of music we go beyond the domain of painting and enter the world of multiple sense imagery.[37] The scene would suggest opera, if opera had ever attempted such a subject.

Before leaving the heavenly sphere to attack the corrupt law courts of Paris, d'Aubigné paints one more spectacular picture involving simultaneously God and the world. He introduces the subject of the Palais de Justice by having God suddenly glance down at the proud and evil building:

> Le Tout-Puissant plana sur le haut de la nuë
> Long temps, jettant le feu & l'ire de sa veuë
> Sur la terre, & voici: le Tout-Voyant ne void,
> En tout ce que la terre en son orgueil avoit,
> Rien si pres de son œil que la brave rencontre
> D'un gros amas de tours qui eslevé se monstre
> Dedans l'air plus hautain. Cet orgueil tout nouveau
> De pavillons dorez faisoit un beau chasteau
> Plein de lustre & d'esclat, dont les cimes pointues,
> Braves, contre le ciel mipartissoyent les nuës.[38]

It is another impressive and splendid composition, with God's downward glance providing the Jacob's ladder motif. In effect the first 175 lines of *La Chambre dorée* form one great theatrical canvass, where human and divine elements are mingled in constant interaction.

36. *La Chambre dorée*, 109–118.
37. See Chapter III, 4.
38. *La Chambre dorèe*, 161–170.

The numerous accounts of martyr's deaths in *Les Feux*, which often deserve attention for their purely theatrical quality, are interesting also for the Jacob's ladder motif. In addressing the martyrs collectively, d'Aubigné exclaims:

Ames dessous l'autel victimes des idoles,
Je preste à vos courroux le fiel de mes paroles,
En attendant le jour que l'Ange delivrant
Vous aille les portaux du paradis ouvrant.[39]

This theme—the delivering angel, the opening of heaven—appears as the climax of most of the martyrdom scenes. Anne Askève cries out, as the flames consume her:

Voici les cieux ouverts, voici son beau visage![40]

At Lady Jane Grey's death,

La lame du bourreau de son sang fut mouillee:
L'ame s'en vole en haut, les Anges gracieux
Dans le sein d'Abraham la ravirent aux cieux.[41]

This last illustration is especially significant. We move without transition from the blood-stained blade of the executioner to the welcoming angels and to Abraham's bosom.

The description of the death of an anonymous feminine victim of the Massacre of St. Bartholomew undergoes a characteristic development:

Sa parole affoiblit, à peine elle profere
Les noms demi-sonnez de sa sœur & sa mere;
D'un visage plus gay elle tourna les yeux
Vers le ciel de son lict, les plante dans les cieux,
Puis, à petits souspirs, l'ame vive s'avance
Et après les regards & après l'esperance.
Dieu ne refusa point la main de cet enfant,
Son œil vid l'œil mourant, le baisa triomphant,
Sa main luy prit la main, & sa derniere haleine
Fuma au sein de Dieu qui, present à sa peine,
Luy soustint le menton, l'esveilla de sa voix;
Il larmoya sur elle, il ferma de ses doigts
La bouche de loüange achevant sa priere,
Baissant des mesmes doigts pour la fin la paupiere:
L'air tonna, le ciel plut, les simples elemens
Sentirent à ce coup tourment des tourmens.[42]

39. *Les Feux*, 53–56.
40. *Les Feux*, 201.
41. *Les Feux*, 278–280.
42. *Les Feux*, 1077–1092.

It should be noted that this scene begins as a realistic drama, pathetic on a purely human level: the weakening voice, the eyes fixed on the tester of the bed. (A characteristic conceit is introduced by the play on the two meanings of "ciel.") [43] Then, with the presence of God, another dimension is added to the drama; and, though the theme is now a supernatural one, even at this point realistic details are not spared: God takes the girl by the hand, kisses her eyes, strokes her chin, and weeps upon her. (The use of such homely detail in representations of the divine is, incidentally, frequently encountered in baroque painting.) The thunder and rain at the close of the story add a final apocalyptic note. There is, in this passage, a fusion of different elements: human and divine, humble and apocalyptic; but the dominant impression is one of theatricality.

It would be possible to multiply almost indefinitely these stories of the dying moments of martyrs; they form virtually the entire subject of the fourth book of *Les Tragiques,* and constitute a significant parallel to representations of the same theme in the fine arts of the period. Such works as Correggio's "Martyrdom of Saints Placidus and Flavia," or Bernini's "Death of the Blessed Ludovica Albertoni," which betray the baroque fondness for fusing the erotic and ecstatic (as discussed in another chapter),[44] are equally valid as examples of theatricality.

However, the most striking illustration of the Jacob's ladder motif remains to be considered. D'Aubigné's narrative of the Massacre of St. Bartholomew undergoes a gradual evolution which corresponds to a most curious sequence of events. In the beginning this account, though highly theatrical, remains on a realistic plane. Although the poet, as we have seen, uses various devices to emphasize the dramatic aspects of his story, it is essentially the description of an actual historical event. This is tragic and sensational history but history nevertheless. The account of the massacre begins on line 705 of *Les Fers* and occupies the reader's attention for nearly five hundred lines. But then, on line 1195, the scene suddenly shifts to heaven and we remember that the whole episode, after all, is one of those vast pictures painted in heaven for the contemplation of the elect. Until line 1447 the poet is engaged in a conversation with an angel in heaven; at this point we return to earth. There follows a fine description of the ocean, noteworthy for rich imagery and splendor. The old god of the ocean, who had been swimming peacefully around his domain, is then introduced. The bodies of the Protestant martyrs hurled into the Seine, the Loire, the Garonne, and the other rivers of France, have stained the waters blood red. The ocean god is indignant at this pollution:

43. It may in fact be argued that the transition from earth to heaven occurs at this point.
44. See Chapter III, 5.

Il trouva cas nouveau, lors que son poil tout blanc
Ensanglanta sa main; puis voyant à son flanc
Que l'onde refuyant laissoit sa peau rougie:
"A moy! dit-il, à moy! pour me charger d'envie,
A moy! qui dans mon sein ne souffre point les morts,
La charogne, l'ordure, ains la jette à mes bords!
Bastardes de la terre & non filles des nues,
Fievres de la nature! Allons, testes cornues
De mes beliers armés, repoussez les, hurtez,
Qu'ils s'en aillent ailleurs purger leurs cruautez."
Ainsi la mer alloit, faisant changer de course
Des gros fleuves à mont vers la coulpable source,
D'où sortoit par leurs bords un deluge de sang.
A la teste des siens, l'Ocean au chef blanc
Vid les cieux s'entrouvrir, & les anges à troupes
Fondre de l'air en bas, ayant en main les coupes
De precieux rubis, qui, plongés dedans l'eau,
En chantant rapportoyent quelque present nouveau.
Ces messagers ailés, ces Anges de lumiere
Trioyent le sang meurtri d'avec l'onde meurtriere
Dans leurs vases remplis, qui prenoyent heureux lieu
Aux plus beaux cabinets du palais du grand Dieu.[45]

The scene ends with the repentance of Neptune, who, dazzled by the sight of the angels, realizes his mistake—

. . . O saincts que je repousse!
Pour vous, non contre vous, juste je me courrouce—

and himself undertakes to go up the Loire in order to gather the bodies of more martyrs. If I have permitted myself to indulge in such an extended quotation, it is because this particular passage first made me realize that *Les Tragiques* might have affinities with baroque art. What had begun on a realistic, historical level, had progressively transformed itself into a spectacular supernatural drama, with classical mythology and Christian legend blended. The blood-red rivers staining the sea, Neptune commanding the rivers to reverse their courses, the opening of the heavens, the descent of hosts of angels bearing ruby chalices to gather up the martyrs' blood—what scene in all of French literature is more suggestive in extravagant, theatrical splendor of the masterpieces of baroque painting? More precisely, it is just such a subject as would have interested Rubens, El Greco, or Tintoretto.

This discussion of the *merveilleux chrétien* in *Les Tragiques* would not be

45. *Les Fers*, 1487-1508.

complete without some mention of the numerous apocalyptic passages in the poem. The Book of Revelation was, in all probability, d'Aubigné's favorite in the Bible; as a member of a persecuted religion he took particular delight in describing God's anger against the unrighteous and in anticipating the Day of Judgment. Typical is the account of the wrath of God when he hears of the iniquities being perpetrated during the religious wars:

> Dieu se leve en courroux & au travers des cieux
> Perça, passa son chef; à l'esclair de ses yeux
> Les cieux se sont fendus; tremblan, suans de crainte,
> Les hauts monts ont croulé: cette majesté saincte
> Paroissant fit trembler les simples elemens,
> Et du monde esbranla les stables fondements.
> Le tonnerre grondant frappa cent fois la nuë:
> Tout s'enfuit, tout s'estonne, & gemit à sa veue
> Les Rois espouvantez laissent choir, paslissans,
> De leurs sanglantes mains les sceptres rougissans; [46]

It is unusual in French poetry to encounter such Miltonic accents. When we read such passages as these in *Les Tragiques,* we cannot help regretting that Boileau's edict banished the *merveilleux chrétien* from the poetry of his country, for we have here evidence that the French genius might have produced a *Divine Comedy* or a *Paradise Lost. Les Feux* ends with another apocalyptic passage, which, though fine, is on the whole inferior to the one just quoted.[47] It is, however, in the final book of *Les Tragiques, Jugement,* that we find the greatest poetry of this kind. When we consider the importance of the Last Judgment as a theme in French medieval art—the portals of Moissac, Autun, Bourges, and Reims come to mind—it is curious that its most powerful expression in French literature does not occur until the late sixteenth century, and then is the work of a Protestant poet.

The opening lines of *Jugement* set the keynote:

> Baisse donc, Eternel, tes hauts cieux pour descendre,
> Frappe les monts cornus, fay-les fumer & fendre;
> Loge le pasle effroy, la damnable terreur
> Dans le sein qui te hait & qui loge l'erreur;
> Donne aux foibles agneaux la salutaire crainte,
> La crainte, & non la peur rende la peur esteinte.[48]

Sporadic quotation cannot do justice to *Jugement;* it would be necessary to reproduce almost the entire book to give an adequate idea of its apocalyptic

---

46. *Le Chambre dorée,* 139–148.
47. Cf. *Les Feux,* 1389–1420.
48. *Jugement,* 1–6.

power. D'Aubigné has sought to give concrete and theatrical expression to the verse from Revelation: "And I saw a new heaven and a new earth: for the first heaven and the first earth were passed away; and there was no more sea." [49] The raising of the dead from their burial places is described with a drama and a realism reminiscent of medieval frescoes:

> C'est fait, Dieu vient regner; de toute prophetie
> Se void la periode à ce poinct accomplie.
> La terre ouvre son sein, du ventre des tombeaux
> Naissent des enterrés les visages nouveaux:
> Du pré, du bois, du champ, presque de toutes places
> Sortent les corps nouveaux & les nouvelles faces.
> Ici les fondemens des chasteaux rehaussés
> Par les ressuscitans promptement sont percés;
> Ici un arbre sent des bras de sa racine
> Grouïller un chef vivant, sortir une poictrine; [50]

Meanwhile, in heaven:

> Un grand Ange s'escrie à toutes nations:
> "Venez respondre ici de toutes actions,
> L'Eternel veut juger." Toutes ames venuës
> Font leurs sieges en rond en la voute des nuës,
> Et là les Cherubins ont au milieu planté
> Un throne rayonnant de saincte majesté.
> Il n'en sort que merveille & qu'ardente lumiere,
> Le soleil n'est pas fait d'une estoffe si claire;
> L'amas de tous vivans en attend justement
> La desolation ou le contentement.[51]

An episode which seems to be wholly original with d'Aubigné (the theme occurs in germinal form in *Les Feux*) [52] takes place when the various elements in nature appear before the judgment seat to testify against the evildoers who have used them for murderous purposes:

> "Pourquoy, dira le feu, avez-vous de mes feux
> Qui n'estoyent ordonnez qu'à l'usage de vie
> Fait des bourreaux, valets de vostre tyrannie?"
> L'air encor une fois contr'eux se troublera,
> Justice au Juge sainct, trouble, demandera
> Disant: "Pourquoi, tyrans & furieuses bestes,
> M'empoisonnastes-vous de charognes, de pestes,

49. Revelation 21:1.
50. *Jugement*, 663–672.
51. *Jugement*, 725–734.
52. Cf. *Les Feux*, 522.

Des corps de vos meurtris?" "Pourquoi, diront les eaux,
Changeastes-vous en sang l'argent de nos ruisseaux?" [53]

For d'Aubigné's account of the joys of the blessed in heaven, we refer the
reader to Chapter III, 4: Multiple Sense Imagery. His description of the
tortures of the damned is, as might be expected, vivid:

> Abbayez comme chiens, hurlez en vos tourmens!
> L'abysme ne respond que d'autres hurlemens.
> Les Satans decouplés d'ongles & dents tranchantes,
> Sans mort, deschireront leurs proyes renaissantes;
> Ces demons tourmentans hurleront tourmentés,
> Leurs fronts seillonneront ferrés de cruautés;
> Leurs yeux estincelans auront la mesme image
> Que vous aviez baignans dans le sang du carnage; [54]

However, their most unbearable torment will be their awareness of the
happiness of the elect:

> . . . . sçavoir aux enfers ce que l'on faict aux cieux,
> Où le camp triomphant gouste l'aise indicible. [55]

The finest passage in *Jugement,* while perhaps not theatrical in the sense of
so many of the illustrations given in this chapter, is undoubtedly one of the
most successful attempts in literature to convey a sense of the drama of the
Last Judgment. Here is d'Aubigné's version of the twenty-fifth chapter of
Matthew:

> "Vous qui m'avez vestu au temps de la froidure,
> Vous qui avez pour moy souffert peine & injure,
> Qui à ma seche soif & à mon aspre faim
> Donnastes de bon cœur vostre eau & vostre pain,
> Venez, race du ciel, venez, esleus du Pere;
> Vos pechés sont esteints, le Juge est vostre frere;
> Venez donc, bien-heureux, triompher pour jamais
> Au royaume eternel de victoire & de paix."
> A ce mot tout se change en beautés éternelles.
> Ce changement de tout est si doux aux fideles!
> Que de parfaits plaisirs! O Dieu, qu'ils trouvent beau
> Cette terre nouvelle & ce grand ciel nouveau!
> Mais d'autre part, si tost que l'Eternel fait bruire
> A sa gauche ces mots, les foudres de son ire,
> Quand ce Juge, & non Pere, au front de tant de Rois
> Irrevocable pousse & tonne cette voix:

53. *Jugement,* 770–778.
54. *Jugement,* 1033–1040.
55. *Jugement,* 1046–1047.

"Vous qui avez laissé mes membres aux froidures,
Qui leur avez versé injures sur injures,
Qui à ma seche soif & à mon aspre faim
Donnastes fiel pour eau & pierre au lieu de pain,
Allez, maudits, allez grincer vos dents rebelles
Au gouffre tenebreux des peines eternelles." [56]

Whatever critical verdict the reader may care to give on the final baroque culmination of the St. Bartholomew episode, this passage at least is ample justification for the use of the *merveilleux chrétien*.

56. *Jugement*, 871–892.

Chapter III: INCARNATION

1. The Concreteness of the Imagery

PROTESTANTS and Catholics have long differed as to the propriety of leading men to feel the presence of God through an appeal to the senses. The former have based their stand upon the commandment: "Thou shalt not make unto thee any graven image, or any likeness of any thing that is in heaven above, or that is in the earth beneath, or that is in the water under the earth." [1] D'Aubigné himself frequently speaks with disapproval of the sensuousness of Catholic ritual, and praises those militant Protestants who destroy graven images or trample upon the Host. The feeling is still reflected in the austerity of worship of many Protestant denominations in present-day America. The half-conscious disapproval which many Americans feel for the arts probably stems from this same religious attitude that physical beauty, because it acts upon the senses, is somehow sinful.

The Catholic view, as reflected in the ritual of the mass or in the masterpieces of Counter Reformation art, is that a love of beautiful things in nature may lead to a love of God. In this, Catholics find themselves close to the doctrine of Plato, as expressed by Diotima to Socrates, that man can, through a love of the beautiful, pass from the concrete to the abstract, from the individual to the universal, and so proceed by steppingstones from earth to heaven.[2]

Yet, when we come to poetic practice, we find d'Aubigné, despite his theology, closer to the Catholic than to the Protestant view. The reader of *Les Tragiques* can hardly fail to be struck with the extreme concreteness of the imagery; and this impression is likely to be all the stronger if he is familiar with the later generations of poets in the seventeenth century. Whereas French classical verse tends toward the abstract expression of ideas and feelings, d'Aubigné, on the other hand, is conspicuous for his use of vivid metaphors to express intangible concepts. In English poetry, from Spenser and Shakespeare and Milton to the present, we have long been accustomed to this procedure; but the Frenchman who comes from the reading of Corneille or Racine is likely to experience displeasure and shock at first contact with d'Aubigné. The imagery in *Les Tragiques* will impress him as unnecessarily physical and consequently in questionable taste.

1. Exodus 20:4.
2. Cf. Plato, *Symposium*, Jowett translation.

Baroque art, however, is incarnational in nature; that is, it seeks to give physical expression to unseen realities. When Bernini wished to communicate the power and authority of the papacy, he designed the great colonnades which surround the piazza and lead up to the façade of St. Peter's in Rome. In an effort to represent the grace of God descending upon Santa Teresa, he contructed actual shiny metal shafts simulating rays of light. An examination of the work of either El Greco or Rubens will reveal an analogous technique: physical flames come down upon the heads of the apostles in the former's "Descent of the Holy Ghost," [3] while the latter's Judgment scenes present a beefy concreteness. The baroque is of course generally associated with the Counter Reformation; and after the Council of Trent the Catholic Church, seeking to stress that very appeal to the senses which the Protestants condemned, designed settings of ever-increasing magnificence for the incarnational drama of the mass. The Gesù in Rome is a characteristic example of the attempt to express religious experience in sensuous and emotional terms. Of the theatrical and propagandistic elements in baroque art much has already been said. It should be repeated, however, that the baroque style is not limited to Catholic artists and writers (Rembrandt and Milton come to mind) and d'Aubigné, though the most militant of Protestants, is sensuous and incarnational in his poetic style.

Complete abstraction is, of course, impossible in poetry; by the very nature of the art some degree of concreteness is inevitable. Let us, however, examine some of d'Aubigné's metaphors and try to discern what kind of imagery appeals to his sensibility.

In the *Préface* to *Les Tragiques* the author explains his poetic intentions and, while deprecating the frivolity of his earlier love poetry, insists upon the higher moral purpose of the present work. He describes his poems as children which he has begotten; although there is nothing very original in this simile, it is significant to note that he develops the imagery at some length, and by the use of specific adjectives gives it a very concrete character. His earlier work, the *Printemps,* is termed "cet enfant bouffon," and then the poet goes on to say:

> Suis-je fascheux de me jouër
> A mes enfans, de les louër?
> Amis, pardonnez-moi ce vice:
> S'ils sont camus & contrefaicts,
> Ni la mere ni la nourrice
> Ne trouvent point leurs enfans laids.[4]

3. In the Prado.
4. *Préface,* 73–78.

If d'Aubigné had contented himself with the banal general statement that
a poet looks upon his poems as a father looks upon his children, there would be
nothing worth noting here; but when the children are depicted as clowns,
snub-nosed or deformed, and the poet *plays* with them, we visualize them
vividly; the abstract concept of the relationship of the author to his work becomes concrete. It is characteristic, also, that these adjectives are essentially
homely rather than poetic in effect; the classical purist will probably be
shocked at the idea of describing a poem as "snub-nosed."

Again discussing his work, d'Aubigné explains early in *Misères* that his
undertaking—an epic poem about the struggles of the Protestant church—has
never before been attempted. He embodies this idea in a prolonged metaphor
which might be summed up in a familiar modern colloquialism: he is blazing
a trail. Once more it must be admitted that there is nothing new about this
trail-blazing image; yet the poet has elaborated it in such a way as to make it
fresh and striking:

> . . . ces chemins enlacez
> Sont par l'antiquité des siecles effacez,
> Si bien que l'herbe verde en ses sentiers acreüe
> En fait une prairie espaisse, haute & druë.
> Là où estoyent les feux des prophetes plus vieux,
> Je tends comme ie puis le cordeau de mes yeux,
> Puis je cours au matin; de ma jambe arrosee,
> J'esparpille à costé la premiere rosee,
> Ne laissant après moi trace à mes successeurs
> Que les reins tous ployez des inutiles fleurs,
> Fleurs qui tombent si tost qu'un vrai soleil les touche,
> Ou que Dieu fenera par le vent de sa bouche.[5]

The comparatively simple image of opening up a path has expanded into a
lush and visual scene; new images have been suggested to the poet's mind as
he writes, and these images in turn have also been developed concretely. In this
connection it should be noted that here we actually watch the progress of the
creative imagination; we witness the growth of the imagery in the poet's consciousness. This interest in the movement of the mind as it discovers new ideas
may also be found in prose writers like Sir Thomas Browne, Montaigne, and
Pascal, as Mr. Croll has pointed in his excellent article on the baroque style in
prose.[6] We are presented not with the finished product of thought but with
thought itself. But to return to the passage from *Misères:* the idea of a path has
suggested to the poet pictures of tall grass and the grass is vividly described
in four adjectives—"verde," "espaisse," "haute," and "druë." D'Aubigné then

5. *Misères*, 23–34.
6. Morris W. Croll, "The Baroque Style in Prose." Cf. Bibliography.

thinks of dew and communicates this image to the reader most strikingly by mentioning his "jambe arrosee." In seeking to express the idea that his purpose is to gather not flowers but fruit, he has been led to dwell on the picture of branches weighted down with blossoms; and then the further image comes to his mind of flowers fading in the sun; finally the sun is likened to the breath of God. We have come a long way from our starting point of trail blazing; but all the images which have grown up in d'Aubigné's imagination are extremely concrete. We began with a metaphoric expression of the idea that *Les Tragiques* is a completely original undertaking; and gradually a landscape has been created before our eyes. Even the simple act of seeing has been transformed into the stretching of a bowstring.

Some of d'Aubigné's metaphors are decidedly less pleasing than the one just quoted. The love of concreteness at times leads him to a heaping-up of physiological details drawn from the medical theories of his century. In order to illustrate the idea that France, in the religious wars, is inwardly destroying herself, he paints the picture of a diseased giant:

> Son corps est combatu, à soi-mesme contraire:
> Le sang pur ha le moins, le flegme & la colere
> Rendent le sang non sang; . . .

> Ce vieil corps tout infect, plein de sa discrasie,
> Hydropique, fait l'eau, si bien que ce geant,
> Qui alloit de ses nerfs ses voisins outrageant,
> Aussi foible que grand n'enfle plus que son ventre.
> Ce ventre dans lequel tout se tire, tout entre,
> Ce faux dispensateur des communs excremens
> N'envoye plus aux bords les justes alimens:
> Des jambes & des bras les os sont sans moelle,
> Il ne va plus en haut pour nourrir la cervelle
> Qu'un chime venimeux dont le cerveau nourri
> Prend matiere et liqueur d'un champignon pourri.[7]

This passage has already been discussed in our study of baroque horror; but it is worth reexamination for the concreteness of its imagery. I do not present it as an example of poetic beauty but feel that its very faults may help us to gain an understanding of d'Aubigné's imagery. Here again the poet has begun by giving concrete expression to a general idea; but he soon allows the physical details to run away with him and indulges to the full his love of graphic representation. This welter of medical details—dropsy, chyle, excrements, marrow, and decaying flesh—is disagreeably vivid; and while it may be less acceptable to the modern reader than the tall grasses, dew, and flowers of the

7. *Misères*, 141–156.

preceding passage it is at least as revelatory of the nature of baroque imagery. As a matter of fact, a majority of the metaphors in *Les Tragiques,* though usually less repulsive in their details than the above, are similarly elaborated into a riot of concreteness. When it occurs to the poet to compare war-torn France to a storm-tossed ship manned by a divided crew, he at once converts the rather conventional simile into a vivid twenty-line scene. As the sea threatens to swallow up the ship or to dash it against the rocks, one band of sailors has seized the bow while the others are ambushed astern; the two factions fire cannon at each other until the ship is blown up and sinks. A little further on in *Misères* a just king is pictured entering a prosperous city in the good old days; this is contrasted with the arrival of a modern tyrant in a ruined and starving city. In the first case, prosperity is expressed in the image of a bursting udder:

> Les villes employent mille & mille artifices
> Pour faire comme font les meilleurs nourrices,
> De qui le sein fecond se prodigue à l'ouvrir,
> Veut montrer qu'il en a pour perdre & pour nourrir.
> Il semble que le pis, quand il est esmeu, voye;
> Il se jette en la main, dont ces meres, de joye,
> Font rejaillir aux yeux de leurs mignons enfans
> Du laict qui leur regorge: . . .[8]

The concept of fertile prosperity is, to say the least, rendered with startling concreteness; especially interesting, however, is the fact that the udder imagery is continued in the succeeding passage and adapted to suit the contrasting picture of the tyrant's entry:

> La ville est un corps mort, il passe sur son ventre,
> Et ce n'est plus du laict qu'elle prodigue en l'air,
> C'est du sang, . . .[9]

Two more examples will serve to complete this discussion of the elaborate and visual character of d'Aubigné's longer metaphors. Both are drawn from *Princes.* In the first,[10] the poet devotes over twenty lines to developing a comparison between kings and mountains. The mountaintops, which are lofty and snow-covered, correspond to the heads of kings, cold, beautiful, and sterile. On the other hand, the mountainsides are covered with rocky precipices, where ferocious lions and tigers and hissing, writhing adders live; these represent the monarchs' vices and bloodthirsty desires. As usual the imagery, though

8. *Misères,* 569–576.
9. *Misères,* 586–588.
10. Cf. *Princes,* 367–390.

created with the original intention of elucidating a complex idea, has developed into a kind of picturesque landscape painting.

The other example is to be found in the closing lines of the same book and, because it is one of d'Aubigné's most successful metaphors, is worth quoting here in its entirety. The poet has been explaining that even innocent and unimportant people living at court are morally responsible for the corruption which they have tacitly accepted. Though perhaps weak and harmless themselves, they have acquiesced in the evil surrounding them and have profited materially through their association with the king. Therefore when the vengeance of God is wrought upon the princes these little people will be destroyed also. This concept becomes another landscape:

> . . . Comme lors que l'esclat
> D'un foudre exterminant vient renverser à plat
> Les chesnes resistans & les cedres superbes,
> Vous verrez là dessous les plus petites herbes,
> La fleur qui craint le vent, le naissant arbrisseau,
> En son nid l'escurieu, en son aire l'oiseau,
> Sous ce daix qui changeoit les gresles en rosee,
> La bauge du sanglier, du cerf la reposee,
> La ruche de l'abeille & la loge au berger
> Avoir eu part à l'ombre, avoir part au danger.[11]

Like many other baroque procedures, the technique of lengthy and detailed metaphor, while at times producing unfortunate and tasteless effects, is also capable of creating passages of great beauty. The specific details accumulated here are, as usual, noteworthy for the strength of their direct visual appeal and the scene as a whole will bear comparison with Ronsard's descriptions of nature in the Vendômois. Whereas in some instances the intensely physical quality of the images in *Les Tragiques* absorbs our attention at the expense of the idea embodied, here we have a harmonious fusion of form and content. When incarnational art does succeed, we have an added dimension of beauty; perhaps that is why this passage may strike some readers as richer than many by Ronsard on similar subjects.

Concreteness of expression is found not only in d'Aubigné's fully developed metaphors but also in his choice of individual words and images. *Princes* begins with a diatribe against the corrupt rulers of France, and the poet characterizes his bitterly satirical verse in the following terms:

> J'en ai rougi pour vous, quand l'acier de mes vers
> Burinoit vostre histoire aux yeux de l'univers.[12]

11. *Princes*, 1517–1526.
12. *Princes*, 20.

The words "acier" and "burinoit" are important here. Not only do they describe very accurately the satire of d'Aubigné but also they are themselves particularly typical of his style. A weaker and more conventional poet might have said "traçait votre portrait," and it is by comparing the words with some such banal expression that we can appreciate their forceful concreteness. We remember such images because they have a sharp bite. Again, when d'Aubigné recalls the wartime conditions under which he writes his verse, while serving in the Protestant armies, he says

> Nous avortons ces chants au milieu des armees.[13]

There is nothing unusual in comparing the act of literary composition to childbirth; those familiar with French scholarly circles know the slang expressions "accoucher" and "pondre"; it is the poet's choice of a specific and violent term like "avortons" that makes the image arresting.

The tyrants who are oppressing France are often described as "allouvis"—they have become werewolves—and the poet tells us that they suck blood through a hole in the sheep's belly, leaving the rest of the body untouched. The cities of France are repeatedly called "charognes"; indeed, though he has written no poem bearing this title, d'Aubigné's preoccupation with the word reminds one of Baudelaire. In order to make vivid the arrogance with which the pope treats the king of France, the poet exclaims:

> . . . on void, sans qu'on s'estonne,
> La pantoufle crotter les lys de la couronne.[14]

I wish here to call attention not so much to the slipper, lilies, and crown, concrete as these images are; it is the verb "crotter" which lifts the expression out of the conventional into the original and striking.

It should by now be evident that d'Aubigné, even more than most poets, thinks in terms of images rather than abstractions, and that his poetic style is characterized by an unusual degree of concreteness. Even the titles of two parts of *Les Tragiques* are significant: they are not "Les Tortures" and "Les Massacres," but *Les Feux* and *Les Fers*. It will be interesting now to examine some of the more particular aspects of d'Aubigné's concreteness.

2. Personification

It is not intended to argue that the use of so traditional a figure of speech as personification is a remarkable trait in d'Aubigné, or that this rhetorical device is in itself a baroque feature; it is felt, however, that the particular way in which this poet uses personification is an important aspect of his style. We

13. *Misères*, 70.
14. *Misères*, 1218.

have seen that d'Aubigné likes to transform abstract ideas into elaborate pictures; his great fondness for personifying in vivid detail virtues, vices, institutions, and countries is really an extension of the same principle. We meet with this device as early as the opening lines of *Misères* and it will repay us to pause and analyze what the poet has done. He has personified the true (in this case, of course, the Protestant) Church. This not very unusual procedure would not detain us if the poet had been content to capitalize the word "Eglise" and to attribute a few human feelings to her. But he has done more:

> Mais dessous les autels des idoles j'advise
> Le visage meurtri de la captive Eglise,
> Qui à sa delivrance (aux despens des hazards)
> M'appelle, m'animant de ses trenchans regards.[15]

As in the case of d'Aubigné's metaphors, we are confronted with a visually striking scene. An abstract idea—the persecution of the reformed faith—is embodied in such a way as to make a direct and dramatic appeal to our eyes. The Church is crushed down under the altars of heathen idols; her face is "meurtri," and her glances are "trenchans." The choice of these two adjectives is important; they are not vague and general but specific and concrete. D'Aubigné's personifications are never mere cold allegorical figures; they strike us by their individuality; they have flesh and blood. We are interested not only in the idea represented but also in the portrait which has been created.

The concept of France torn by civil war is also personified with considerable vigor. The brutality of the imagery will probably be offensive to some readers; but though one may question the good taste of the following scene, its vividness is undeniable. D'Aubigné is addressing France personified, and the two opposing religions are represented as her two children:

> Tu leur donnes la vie, & dessous ta mammelle
> S'esmeut des obstinez la sanglante querelle;
> Sur ton pis blanchissant ta race se debat,
> Là le fruict de ton flanc faict le champ du combat."
> Je veux peindre la France une mere affligee,
> Qui est entre ses bras de deux enfans chargee.
> Le plus fort, orgueilleux, empoigne les deux bouts
> Des tetins nourriciers; puis, à force de coups
> D'ongles, de poings, de pieds, il brise le partage
> Dont nature donnoit à son besson l'usage; [16]

The important part played by scenes of violence, sadism, and terror in *Les Tragiques* has already been discussed in another chapter, and this same pas-

15. *Misères*, 13–16.
16. *Misères*, 93–102.

sage has been offered as an example of d'Aubigné's fondness for horrifying metaphor. It is, however, no less interesting as a specimen of his handling of personification. The poet has gone far beyond conventional personification; France and her two children have been made much more physical than ordinary allegorical figures. France's breasts are emphasized in three different terms: "mamelle," "pis," and "tetins." We have no mere theoretical conflict here but a "sanglante querelle," in which the stronger child strikes blows with his nails, fists, and feet. For an artistic parallel to this kind of personification we should look not to classical or Renaissance statuary but to canvasses of Rubens like the Medici series in the Louvre, or his "Triumph of the Eucharist" in the Prado.

Of course, in the preceding example (not, by the way, given in its entirety) the personifications receive an exceptionally full development, with a riot of striking details, but often in *Les Tragiques* even the most passing reference to a concept or a moral trait calls up images of living flesh and blood. Thus in *Princes,*

> . . . la verité bannie,
> Meurtrie & deschiree, est aux prisons, aux fers.[17]

Vanity, in the same scene, is using every possible means to chase Truth away, and

> La pauvrette soustient mille playes au corps.

Truth, which most people would regard as a highly abstract concept, has here been endowed with such physical reality that she is bruised and torn, cast into chains, and gashed with a thousand wounds. An idea has become so incarnate that it acts painfully upon the reader's senses. D'Aubigné's personifications, like his metaphors, have a bite to them.

One of the most elaborate allegories in the whole of *Les Tragiques* occurs toward the end of *Princes,* when Fortune and Virtue hold the stage for some three hundred lines.[18] The innocent young man who has come to the dissolute court of the Valois, horrified by the vices he has seen, has retired to his room and to bed. Fortune, appearing to him in a vision, makes a long, cynical speech of worldly advice. She makes her entrance amid a glow of yellowish-brown light and wears a coat of mail. Accompanying her are two naked, blindfolded children, who jump up on the bed and start playing with the fringe. Fortune, thrusting apart the curtains, falls upon the youth, hugging and kissing him madly. Her harangue of immoral advice continues for 126 lines; at this point Virtue, who has been listening at the keyhole, is overcome with indignation

17. *Princes,* 162–163.
18. *Princes,* 1180–1486.

and bursts into the room. Fortune is struck dumb, her "moonlight" obliterated by Virtue's "sunlight"; she and the two naked children instantly change into demons, then into smoke, then into wind, then into nothingness. Virtue meanwhile, who is dressed as a matron, takes a chair and places it by the head of the young man's bed; she grasps his trembling hand, gives him a chaste kiss, and embarks on 151 lines of sound moral advice. This scene is a curious one in several ways; d'Aubigné's interest in demons and metamorphoses is discussed elsewhere. At first sight, we may be struck primarily by the supernatural and theatrical happenings: Fortune's appearance in a glow of sulphurous light, her dramatic disappearance into demons and smoke; and these elements undeniably contribute to the vividness of the scene. However, we are concerned here with the manner in which the poet makes his personifications seem to be living beings. The two portraits are, as a matter of fact, individualized and contrasted: Fortune thrusts the bed curtains asunder and smothers the boy in kisses; Virtue, on the contrary, sits on a chair at his bedside, takes him comfortingly by the hand, and gives him a motherly kiss. Because of these details, instead of merely apprehending intellectual concepts, we actually visualize women of flesh and blood.

It is *La Chambre dorée,* however, that offers this rhetorical device in greatest profusion. The description of the Paris law courts gives d'Aubigné an opportunity to enumerate all the vices which are to be found there; as might be expected, he does not fail to indulge his love of allegory. Over six hundred lines of this book are essentially a catalogue of every conceivable human vice and weakness. Most readers, with considerable justification, have found the passage tiresome; but, as has already been seen, frequently those parts of *Les Tragiques* which are of inferior poetic merit give the critic a valuable insight into d'Aubigné's methods. The poet lists the following sins as present in the law courts: injustice, avarice, ambition, wrath, favoritism, drunkenness, hypocrisy, vindictiveness, fickleness, stupidity, ignorance, cruelty, passion, hatred, servility, clownishness, lust, weakness, laziness, youthful indiscretion, treachery, insolence, legal formalism, fear, and *hubris;* and every one of these undesirable traits is given a vivid living embodiment.

Despite the cataloguelike quality of this section of the poem, some of the individual portraits in the gallery are striking. Consider, for instance, this one:

> A gauche avoit seance une vieille harpie
> Qui entre ses genoux grommeloit accroupie,
> Comptoit et recomptoit, aprochoit de ses yeux
> Noirs, petits, enfoncez, les dons plus precieux
> Qu'elle recache es plis de sa robe rompue:
> Ses os en mille endroits repoussans sa chair nue,

> D'ongles rouillez, crochus, son tappi tout cassé
> A tout propos panchant par elle estoit dressé.
> L'Avarice en mangeant est toujours affamee.[19]

This is the portrait of an individual, not a bare abstraction. The specific details give life and individuality to the picture; for example, d'Aubigné has the old hag hold the coins very close to her sunken eyes as she counts. Her identity is revealed at the end of the passage—a procedure followed in a good many of the personifications in *La Chambre dorée*. These climax-disclosures constitute an important part of the technique of surprise, which is discussed elsewhere. But here their function is largely to permit d'Aubigné to build up a concrete picture before introducing an abstract concept. In this way, the physical reality of the character gets established in the reader's mind ahead of the allegory.

The portrait of drunkenness is also vivid:

> Comment d'un pas douteux en la troupe bacchante,
> Estourdie au matin, sur le soir violante,
> Porte dans le senat un tixon enflambé,
> Folle au front cramoisi, nez rouge, teint plombé,
> Comment l'Yvrongnerie en la foulle eschauffee,
> N'oyant les douces voix, met en pieces Orfee,
> A l'esclat des cornets d'un vineux Evoüé
> Bruit un arrest de mort d'un gosier enroüé! [20]

The abundance of accurate, homely details should be noted. Drunkenness is dazed by hangover in the morning, but violent at night; she is staggering, her nose is red, her complexion sallow, and her voice hoarse; she *belches* as she pronounces a death sentence. By these touches the poet transforms his personification into a physical reality. Throughout his allegorical portrait gallery, d'Aubigné insists on the individual bodily characteristics of the Sins. Ignorance has small, fleshy eyes and a huge mouth; Stupidity, potbellied, is called a pachyderm; Cruelty is a Moor with thick lips; Vanity has effeminate gestures and smells like a prostitute; Lust is bald and has watery eyes. The technique reminds us of Milton's "laughter holding both his sides"; [21] the poet selects a few characteristic physical details which make his personifications live and breathe before our eyes. An artistic style which constantly strives to make ideas visible may justly be termed incarnational.

3. REDNESS AND RADIANCE

In any direct appeal to the senses, color is likely to play an important part. The artist who wishes to stir the feelings as well as the intellect of the beholder

19. *La Chambre dorée*, 249–257.
20. *La Chambre dorée*, 309–316.
21. *L'Allegro*, 32. Cf. also the abstractions in *Comus*, 107–109.

is naturally led to make use of vivid colors. This principle was clearly understood by the majority of baroque painters—men such as Rubens or Tintoretto, El Greco or Van Dyck. Since, in the late sixteenth and seventeenth centuries, the boundaries between different arts often tended to become blurred, it is not surprising to find a poet borrowing this feature of painting and striving to suggest intensity of color in words. Just as Rubens, by the use of scarlet and crimson, conveys impressions of splendor or cruelty, and El Greco by dazzling light expresses the presence of the divine, so d'Aubigné, for similar purposes, delights in images of redness or radiance. Because of the poet's insistence on intense sensations, strong colors are everywhere apparent in *Les Tragiques;* but these two hues deserve special consideration.

Even a casual reader of d'Aubigné's poem can hardly fail to notice the prevalence of red. Usually it is a question of the redness of fire or blood; the color is invoked for its suggestion of violence and its power to arrest the reader's attention. Catherine de' Medici and the Cardinal of Lorraine are referred to as "cramoisis flambeaux"; and in describing the evil deeds of the former, the poet says

> La loingtaine province & l'esloigné clocher
> Par toy sont peints de rouge, . . .[22]

The portrait of the cardinal is a symphony in red:

> Ce cardinal sanglant, couleur à point suivie
> Des desirs, des effects, & pareill'à sa vie:
> Il fut rouge de sang de ceux qui au cercueil
> Furent hors d'aage mis, tuez par son conseil;
> Et puis le cramoisi encores nous avise
> Qu'il a dedans son sang trempé sa paillardise,[23]

Red seems to have for d'Aubigné a symbolic significance. It stands for passion, violence, and cruelty. In general, whenever these themes are stressed in *Les Tragiques,* redness is emphasized as well. The insistence on this color is still another aspect of the concreteness of the imagery, which seeks to give ideas visual representation.

In the catalogue of vices in *La Chambre dorée,* red is the color of Wrath, who is called

> L'Ire empourpree: il sort un feu qui donne horreur
> De ses yeux ondoyans, comme au travers la glace
> D'un chrystal se peut voir d'un gros rubi la face;
> Elle a dans la main droitte un poignard asseché
> De sang qui ne s'efface; . . .[24]

22. *Misères*, 840–841.
23. *Misères*, 997–1002.
24. *La Chambre dorée*, 296–300.

Purple, fire, ruby, blood—d'Aubigné's fondness for this color, and the moral significance which he attaches to it, are unmistakable. In the portrait of Drunkenness, red is also much in evidence: her forehead and nose are red, and she is carrying a flaming firebrand.

Since the subject of *Les Fers* is the massacre of Protestants, d'Aubigné has numerous opportunities to paint in bloody tints. Nearly all the rivers of France are depicted as crimson with blood. At Amboise,

> Entre les condamnés un esleve sa face
> Vers le ciel, luy monstrant le sang fumant et chaud
> Des premiers etestés, puis s'escria tout haut,
> Haussant les mains du sang des siens ensanglantees: [25]

This is only one of the innumerable sanguinary scenes in *Les Tragiques;* of the horrible as a poetic theme much has already been said, but here the threefold repetition of the blood image should be particularly noticed: the poet's intention is clearly to produce a pictorial effect.

The most fully developed picture of bloodshed in *Les Fers* is, of course, the description of the Massacre of St. Bartholomew. The introduction to this section begins immediately to stress the theme of redness:

> Jour qui avec horreur parmi les jours se conte,
> Qui se marque de rouge & rougit de sa honte.
> L'aube se veut lever, aube qui eut jadis
> Son teint brunet orné des fleurs du paradis;
> Quand, par son treillis d'or, la rose cramoisie
> Esclatoit, on disoit: "Voici ou vent, ou pluye."
> Cett'aube, que la mort vient armer & coiffer
> D'estincelans brasiers ou de tisons d'enfer,
> Pour ne dementir point son funeste visage
> Fit ses vents de soupirs, & de sang son orage.[26]

The choice of such a variety of images suggesting redness—blushing, a crimson rose, braziers, firebrands, and blood—is clearly intentional, done for purposes of pictorial symbolism; the tone is set for the crimson and scarlet painting of St. Bartholomew's Day itself. And here, redness appears several times on every page, from the crimson banner flying on the Palais de Justice to the blood-drenched beds and the bleeding fragments of bodies. The Seine holds more blood than water. Men whose hands are not red from bloodshed are seized with false shame:

> Il n'est garçon, enfant, qui quelque sang n'espanche
> Pour n'estre veu honteux s'en aller la main blanche.[27]

25. *Les Fers*, 356–359.
26. *Les Fers*, 769–778.
27. *Les Fers*, 849–850.

The fact that the image of the white hand has been introduced, and set off in contrast with the blood in the preceding line, shows that d'Aubigné was consciously thinking of the *redness* of the picture.

The closing scene in *Les Fers,* where angels descend from heaven to gather up the bodies of the martyrs from the sea, is interesting in another connection —that of the supernatural and spectacular—but it is also noteworthy for its images of redness. Father Ocean is swimming around peacefully when the slaughtered bodies of the Protestants begin to flow into the sea from the rivers of France:

> Il trouva cas nouveau, lors que son poil tout blanc
> Ensanglanta sa main; puis voyant à son flanc
> Que l'onde refuyant laissoit sa peau rougie: [28]

Once more the whiteness of Ocean's beard serves to set off the redness of the blood. The rivers are pouring a "deluge de sang" into the sea when hosts of angels descend from the heavens carrying ruby goblets to gather up the blood. There follows a curious image, based on the sixteenth-century belief in rainstorms of blood:

> Le Soleil . . .
> Ores de chauds rayons exhale à soy le sang
> Qu'il faut qu'en rouge pluye il renvoye à son rang.[29]

Space permits the inclusion of only a few of these red pictures: the reader need only pick up the text to find many more. The words "rouge," "cramoisi," and "escarlate," as well as references to fire and blood, constitute a recurring theme throughout the whole of *Les Tragiques.* The baroque predilection for this color has been noted. The brilliant red costumes in Rubens' painting of "The Head of Cyrus Brought to Queen Tomyris" [30] serve, as so often with d'Aubigné, to emphasize the feeling of cruelty and violence. In the case of El Greco red is also frequently used to express passion or intensity of religious feeling (for example, the red robes in the Munich "Despoiling of Christ" or the Frick Gallery "St. Jerome"). With its intense color, the style of d'Aubigné reveals an affinity with the painting of his age.

In his analysis of the seventeenth-century religious lyric [31] Hatzfeld has called attention to the imagery of light. He considers the prevalence of words like "lumière," "briller," and "éclat" in descriptions of heaven a baroque motif. It should be observed that d'Aubigné likewise visualizes God in terms of light. In keeping with his usual procedure of expressing unseen realities concretely,

28. *Les Fers,* 1487–1489.
29. *Les Fers,* 1509–1511.
30. In the Boston Museum.
31. Hatzfeld, "Der Barockstil der religiösen klassischen Lyrik in Frankreich."

he employs images of brilliance whenever he wishes us to feel the presence of God. As early as the *Préface* to *Les Tragiques*, religious truth is described as a kind of radiance. Setting forth the purposes of his poem, d'Aubigné says:

> Je cerchois de mes tristes yeux
> La verité aux aspres lieux,
> Quand de cett'obscure taniere,
> Je vis resplendir la clarté,
> Sans qu'il y eust autre lumiere:
> Sa lumiere estoit sa beauté.[32]

The words "resplendir" and "clarté," as well as the repetition of "lumière," are characteristic. The light is all the more striking because, in a kind of chiaroscuro effect, it is made to shine in the darkness. The impression is akin to that produced by two famous baroque paintings: El Greco's "Adoration of the Shepherds"[33] and Rembrandt's "Christ and the Pilgrims at Emaus."[34] In both these pictures the light proceeds, not from any natural source, but from Christ Himself; the radiance, which shines forth into an outer darkness, is viewed as a symbol of the divine.

When, in the opening scene of *La Chambre dorée*, Justice, Piety, and Peace come pleading to the throne of God and describe the sufferings of France, the picture glows with brilliant light:

> A ces mots intervient la blanche Pieté,
> Qui de la terre ronde au haut du ciel vouté
> En courroux s'envola; de ses luisantes ailes
> Elle accreut la lueur des voutes eternelles;[35]

Not only is Piety white, with gleaming wings, but the vaults of heaven are conceived of as shining with light. In the same episode, the souls of the elect are

> Pures dans les cieux purs, le beau pays des ames[36]

while the angels of light sing. Solomon's throne is decorated with twelve lions of dazzling metal; the faithful, who see it erected in heaven, are dazzled but themselves walk in splendor and brilliance.

The theme of gleaming whiteness appears in the opening lines of *Les Feux*. In this grandiose scene, the victors of Zion enter marching; they

> Portans l'escharpe blanche ont pris le caillou blanc.[37]

32. *Préface*, 134–138.
33. Metropolitan Museum, New York.
34. Louvre.
35. *La Chambre dorée*, 55–58.
36. *La Chambre dorée*, 114.
37. *Les Feux*, 4.

These two images—the white robes and the white stone—come from Revelation, d'Aubigné's favorite book in the Bible; but his choice of them is none the less significant. White horses, which are also a symbol of salvation in Revelation, are present. In a very characteristic line, the poet exclaims:

> Les feux qui vous brusloyent vous ont rendus candides.[38]

Here the theme of redness and fire comes to join that of whiteness; and the idea of transformation or metamorphosis, of which d'Aubigné is so fond, is likewise in evidence. The adjective "candides," while retaining its etymological sense of "white," has at the same time a figurative suggestion of purity, so that visual imagery and spiritual significance are united in the same word.

D'Aubigné makes the salvation of the Protestant martyrs, at the end of *Les Feux*, visible by the use of the same light imagery. The passage is a notable example of the attempt to make a spiritual state perceptible in concrete terms. A few images of redness are present but in general radiance predominates. Nature, the poet says, has clothed the elect with angelic beauty; and he then introduces one of his elaborate metaphors:

> Ainsi le beau soleil monstre un plus beau visage
> Faisant un soutre clair sous l'espais du nuage,
> Et se faict par regrets, & par desirs, aimer
> Quand les rayons du soir plongent en la mer.
> On dit du pelerin, quand de son lict il bouge,
> Qu'il veut le matin blanc & avoir le soir rouge:
> Vostre naissance, enfance, ont eu le matin blanc,
> Vostre coucher heureux rougit en vostre sang.
> Beautés, vous avanciez d'où retournoit Moyse
> Quand sa face parut si claire et si exquise.
> D'entre les couronnés le premier couronné
> De tels rayons se vid le front environné:
> Tel, en voyant le ciel, fut veu ce grand Estienne
> Quand la face de Dieu brilla dedans la sienne.
> O astres bien-heureux, qui rendez à nostre œil
> Ses miroirs & rayons, lunes du grand soleil![39]

Throughout this passage, light is used as a symbol of the grace of God, and the poet has been ingenious in working out variations of his imagery. First of all, there is the sunset, which with its mixture of redness and light stands for the ideas of martyrdom and salvation. The face of Moses is "claire" and "exquise"; the foreheads of the crowned martyrs are surrounded with rays of light; the countenance of God shines reflected in the face of St. Stephen;

38. *Les Feux*, 14.
39. *Les Feux*, 1269–1284.

and finally, the elect are compared to happy stars or moons, transmitting to our eyes the sunlight of God.

This imagery is maintained consistently throughout *Les Tragiques* whenever d'Aubigné wishes to embody in pictorial form the idea of God. *Les Fers* also begins with a celestial scene, and once more the poet heaps up words suggestive of whiteness and gleaming light. God's head in "rayonné" and heaven is an ivory palace. God Himself is conceived of as the sun, the source of all light:

> Les habitans du ciel comparurent à l'œil
> Du grand soleil du monde, & de ce beau soleil
> Les Seraphins ravis le contemployent à veuë;
> ˙Les Cherubins couverts (ainsi′que d'une nuë)
> L'adoroyent sous un voile; un chacun en son lieu
> Exstatic reluisoit de la face de Dieu.[40]

The light of God is so intense that the cherubim have to veil their eyes in order to look at Him; and all the inhabitants of heaven, in their ecstasy, are glowing with the radiance which proceeds from His face.

One final illustration, from *Jugement,* will complete this discussion of light. In the description of God's appearance at the Last Judgment, the motif of radiance, as befits so apocalyptic a scene, is given exceptional emphasis:

> Dieu paroist: le nuage entre luy & nos yeux
> S'est tiré à l'escart, il s'est armé de feux;
> Le ciel neuf retentit du son de ses louanges;
> L'air n'est plus que rayons tant il est semé d'anges,
> Tout l'air n'est qu'un soleil; le soleil radieux
> N'est qu'une noire nuict au regard de ses yeux,
> Car il brusle le feu, au soleil il esclaire,
> Le centre n'a plus d'ombre & ne fuit sa lumiere.[41]

(For the fuller comprehension of this passage, it should be noted that the phrase "le soleil radieux" refers to the material sun which we know in this world; it is completely eclipsed by the radiance of the heavenly host.)

For artistic parallels, in the baroque period to this use of dazzling light as a symbol of the divine presence, we have already pointed to El Greco's "Nativity" and Rembrandt's "Emaus." There are hosts of other examples. Rembrandt's "Philemon and Baucis" is interesting because the subject here is not the Christian God but two pagan deities.[42] The work of El Greco is full of this supernatural light; a specially interesting case is the Cadiz picture of St.

40. *Les Fers,* 27–32.
41. *Jugement,* 717–724.
42. I.e. Jupiter and Mercury.

Francis with Brother Rufus, because here the two friars seem to be physically dazzled by the divine radiance; Brother Rufus' gesture indicates that he is shielding his eyes. Barocci's painting of the stigmatization of St. Francis [43] also represents God as a dazzling light, and here there is no doubt whatever that the attendant friar is warding off the intense glare with his arm. The apse and ceiling paintings in Roman baroque churches, by Pozzo and Cortona, depict heavenly apotheoses in terms of brilliant light, the effect of which is enhanced by golden windows. Thus, both in literature and in the arts, the baroque style seeks to express God in terms of radiance.

4. MULTIPLE SENSE IMAGERY

It may seem strange that the style of so militantly Protestant a writer as Agrippa d'Aubigné may be elucidated by a study of the *Spiritual Exercises* of St. Ignatius Loyola. However, as Mr. Austin Warren points out in his book on Richard Crashaw, the influence of the *Spiritual Exercises* was profound throughout Europe. We have seen that d'Aubigné, though a Protestant, does not scorn to appeal to his reader's senses; the poetry of *Les Tragiques* resorts constantly to concrete imagery in order to express religious ideas. As a means of literary and artistic expression, the baroque style transcended the national boundaries of Europe; baroque sensibility dominated the minds of men in the late sixteenth and early seventeenth centuries, regardless of their nationality. Similarly, though the baroque is frequently looked upon as basically an art of the Counter Reformation, in reality Protestants as well as Catholics expressed their ideas in this style.

St. Ignatius recommended men to seek God through an application of all their senses: sight, hearing, smell, taste, and touch. Reflecting their author, the *Spiritual Exercises* are extraordinarily systematic and may even strike the modern reader as mechanical. The disciple is supposed to focus each of the five senses in turn upon certain subjects of religious meditation. For instance, the *Fifth Exercise* of the *First Week* is a meditation on hell. We are to experience hell with great concreteness:

The first point will be to see with the eye of the imagination those great fires, and those souls as it were in bodies of fire.

The second, to hear with the ears lamentations, howlings, cries, blasphemies against Christ our Lord and against all His Saints.

The third, with the sense of smell, to smell smoke, brimstone, refuse and rottenness.

The fourth, to taste with the taste bitter things, as tears, sadness, and the worm of conscience.

43. Florence, Uffizi.

The fifth, to feel with the sense of touch how those fires do touch and burn souls.

This step-by-step procedure of applying the senses may be found in many other sections of the *Spiritual Exercises*. Thus, the *Fifth Contemplation* of the *Second Week* consists in training the five senses on the first and second contemplations, which were the Incarnation and the Nativity. Let us see how this works:

The first point is to see the persons with the sight of the imagination, meditating and studying in particular their circumstances, and gathering some fruit from the sight.

The second, to hear with the hearing the things that they say, or may say, and reflecting within oneself to gather thence some profit.

The third, to smell and taste with the sense of smell and taste the infinite fragrance and sweetness of the Godhead, of the soul and its virtues, and of everything, according to the person one is contemplating, reflecting inwardly and gathering thence profit.

The fourth, to touch with the touch, as for instance to embrace and kiss the place where such persons tread and sit, always contriving to gather profit thence.

The technique of acting on several or all of the senses, either at once or in rapid succession, has its counterpart in baroque literary imagery. Mr. Warren has shown that Crashaw is fond of words like "sweet," which combines fragrance and taste, and that much of his imagery appeals simultaneously to several senses.

The same, as we shall see, is true of d'Aubigné; and this aspect of his style I shall term "multiple sense imagery." In most cases, d'Aubigné does not carry the technique as far as Baudelaire and the symbolists. In *Les Tragiques* there is seldom actual "correspondence" between the senses, such as may be seen in Baudelaire's *Correspondances*, Rimbaud's *Vowel Sonnet*, or the liqueur-organ in Huysmans' *A Rebours*. Except for some special cases I have, therefore, rejected the term synesthesia to describe this form of imagery. Some of the pictures painted by d'Aubigné may, indeed, by their compactness produce in the mind sense transferences which border on synesthesia; but his more usual method is to appeal to several senses in succession.

Irving Babbitt, in *The New Laokoon*, has examined at some length the question of the confusion of the arts. It is interesting to observe that this critic, as early as 1910, was aware that the question is related to the baroque problem, for in a note he states:

If I were attempting a complete survey, I should need to take a glance at certain aspects of the baroque and rococo styles, etc. A wider survey of this kind would furnish fresh illustrations of the pseudo-classic tendency to confuse the arts formally and objectively (usually in terms of painting). The man who did more than any one else to confound the standards of painting with those of sculpture and architecture was of course Bernini . . .[44]

We have already seen that the art of *Les Tragiques,* by virtue of its theatricality, has certain affinities with opera; the analogy will gain still further validity when we consider d'Aubigné's multiple sense imagery.

A passage from *Misères* concerning Catherine de' Medici will serve as a first illustration of the technique. Just as St. Ignatius applies the various senses in turn, hoping to lead the faithful to the fear of hell and the love of God, so d'Aubigné is eager to have his readers feel, through smell, touch, sight, and hearing, his own fanatical hatred for Catherine:

> Elle infecte le ciel par la noire fumee
> Qui sort de ses nareaux; ell'haleine les fleurs:
> Les fleurs perdent d'un coup la vie & les couleurs;
> Son toucher est mortel, la pestifere tuë
> Les païs tous entiers de sa basilique vuë;
> Elle change en discord l'accord des elements.
> En paisible minuict on oit ses hurlements,
> Ses sifflements, ses cris, alors que l'enragee
> Tourne la terre en cendre, & en sang l'eau changee.[45]

We smell Catherine's foul breath and see the flowers fade; we feel her touch and her glance to be deadly and hear her howl in the middle of the night. The imagery here is very much more concrete than if visual impressions only were called into play; and the power of the passage as a whole depends upon the combination of four senses.

In speaking of the sadistic amusements of the princes, in the second book of *Les Tragiques,* d'Aubigné, referring to the bloody murders which make even their perpetrators' hair stand on end, exclaims:

> Les œuvres de leurs mains, quoi qu'ils soyent impiteux
> Feront dresser d'horreur & tomber leurs cheveux,
> Transis en leurs plaisirs! O que la playe est forte
> Qui mesm'empuantit le pourri qui la porte![46]

We feel the bristling hair empathically in our sense of touch; the image of a wound conveys impressions of both sight and feeling, while smell is immediately introduced in the following line. Thus in a remarkably short space the poet acts upon three of the reader's senses. A few lines further along, still discussing the pleasures of the princes, he says:

44. *Op. cit.,* p. 58, n. 2.
45. *Misères,* 890–898.
46. *Princes,* 199–202.

Mais ces fleurs secheront, & le sang recelé
Sera puant au nez, non aux yeux revelé: [47]

In these two examples the compactness of the imagery tends to lead to actual sense transference, as with the symbolists of the nineteenth century, so that both passages border on true synesthesia.

The orgies of the evil judges in *La Chambre dorée* become the occasion of another lush description which unites images of taste, smell, touch, and sight:

Ils hument à long traits dans leurs couppes dorees
Suc, laict, sang & sueur des vefves esplorees;
Leur barbe s'en parfume, & aux fins des repas,
Yvres, vont degouttant cette horreur contre bas.
De si aspres forfaicts l'odeur n'est point si forte
Qu'ils ne facent dormir leur conscience morte
Sur des matras enflez du poil des orphelins;
De ce piteux duvet leurs oreillers sont pleins.[48]

It might even be argued that the fifth sense—that of hearing—is contained by implication in the word "esplorees." D'Aubigné's purpose here, as so often throughout his poem, is to shock the reader into indignation; but his stylistic method is in many ways comparable to the Jesuit attempt to arouse religious fervor through the successive application of the senses.

The personification of Drunkenness, cited as an example of the poet's use of the color red, will be remembered; the passage offers an interesting example of multiple sense imagery too, since the visual picture of staggering, red-nosed Yvrongnerie is accompanied by belching, trumpet blasts, and bacchic cries of Evoé! Similarly, Vanity is characterized not only by coy smiles and effeminate gestures but also by lascivious perfumes. The picture of Treachery involves several senses too:

Sa peau de sept couleurs fait des taches sans conte.
De voix sonore & douce & d'un ton feminin
La magique en l'oreille verse son venin.[49]

One of d'Aubigné's favorite instruments of torture, mentioned three times in *Les Tragiques*, probably interests him for reasons of synesthesia: it is the bronze bull of Phalaris, in which victims were burned to death while a special steam device played music to cover up their cries. Elsewhere, the fortress of the Spanish Inquisition is described as both dark and stinking.[50]

La Chambre dorée does not contain only a catalogue of evil: there is also a

47. *Princes*, 215–216.
48. *La Chambre dorée*, 213–219.
49. *La Chambre dorée*, 466–468.
50. *La Chambre dorée*, 531.

portrait gallery of good judges. The Judgment of Solomon, in particular, is vividly depicted: when the Jewish king orders that the child be cut in two,

> On void l'enfant en l'air par deux soldats suspendre,
> L'affamé coutelas qui brille pour le fendre,[51]

Here three different senses are introduced in the space of a single line. The cutlass is thought of as hungry and eager to taste the child; the shining of the blade strikes our eyes; and the word "fendre" makes us feel the wounding of flesh. Inasmuch as the threefold imagery is virtually simultaneous, it may not be inappropriate to speak of synesthesia.

Just before paraphrasing Psalm 58 at the end of *La Chambre dorée*, the poet addresses himself threateningly to evil judges and warns them of the imminent wrath of God. Images of reading (i.e. seeing), tasting, and hearing are successively created:

> Lisez, persecuteurs, le reste de mes chants,
> Vous y pourrez gouster le breuvage aux meschants:
> Mais, aspics, vous avez pour moy l'oreille close.[52]

Probably the closest parallel to St. Ignatius Loyola's application of the five senses is to be found in the description of the delights of heaven, at the end of *Jugement*. There is no doubt that d'Aubigné thought of heaven as a thoroughly material place, where the pleasures were of a physical nature. The satisfactions of each sense are enumerated as systematically as in the *Spiritual Exercises*. However surprising it may seem, the grim Huguenot actually wishes us to see, hear, taste, smell, and feel what salvation is like:

> En mieux il tournera l'usage des cinq sens.
> Veut-il souëfve odeur? Il respire l'encens
> Qu'offrit Jesus en croix, qui en donnant sa vie
> Fut le prestre, l'autel, & le temple & l'hostie.
> Faut-il des sons? Le Grec qui jadis s'est vanté
> D'avoir ouï les cieux, sur l'Olympe monté,
> Seroit ravi plus haut quand cieux, orbes & poles
> Servent aux voix des Saincts de luths & de violes.
> Pour le plaisir de voir les yeux n'ont point ailleurs
> Veu pareilles beautés ni si vives couleurs.
> Le goust, qui fit cercher des viandes estranges,
> Aux nopces de l'Agneau trouve le goust des Anges,
> Nos mets delicieux tousjours prests sans aprets,
> L'eau du rocher d'Oreb, & le Man tousjours frais:
> Nostre goust, qui à soy est si souvent contraire,

---

51. *La Chambre dorée*, 725–726.
52. *La Chambre dorée*, 1001–1003.

Ne goustera l'amer doux ni la douceur amere.
Et quel toucher peut estre en ce monde estimé
Au prix des doux baisers de ce Fils bien aimé? [53]

I think the reader will agree that this is an altogether remarkable passage. Literary descriptions of heaven are, as a rule, less successful than descriptions of hell; and d'Aubigné himself is more famous for expressing terror than bliss; but paradise has seldom been rendered with more concrete sensuousness than here. Intellectually, it may be thought that this picture of heaven is too physical; but artistically, as a symphony of the five different senses, the effect is powerful. The verse of d'Aubigné nearly always produces an impression of vigorous flesh and blood, compared to which the works of many other poets may seem pale and thin; one key to this phenomenon may be found in passages such as this, where all our senses are appealed to at once. Looking again at the *Spiritual Exercises* we can see that the emotional and artistic sensibility of d'Aubigné is perhaps not very different from that of Loyola and other Jesuits; however separated they may be in matters of religious doctrine, they participate artistically in the same *Zeitgeist*. This is the age, it should be repeated, which gave birth to the art form most concerned with a multiple appeal to the senses—opera.

The last two lines describing the joys of heaven reveal another aspect of d'Aubigné's art so important that it must be treated separately.

5. THE EROTIC-ECSTATIC

In the baroque age men expressed the love of God in strongly human terms. We have just seen that d'Aubigné counts the kisses of Christ among the blessings of heaven; and while this mode of expression seems startling to modern taste, there is no doubt that it was thoroughly congenial to baroque sensibility. The poetry of Crashaw, for instance, though deeply sincere in its religious feeling, at times strikes the twentieth-century reader as shockingly erotic in its imagery. One of the finest poems in *Carmen Deo Nostro* is entitled "Prayer: an Ode Which Was Prefixed to a Little Prayer-Book Given to a Young Gentlewoman." The subject is the love of God; yet the wording would be appropriate for a very physical and human love:

O fair! O fortunate! O rich! O dear!
O happy and thrice-happy she,
Dear selected dove,
Whoe'er she be
Whose early love

> With wingèd vows
> Makes haste to meet her morning Spouse
> And close with his immortal kisses.

The poem, after mentioning "bottomless treasures Of pure inebriating pleasures," closes with the following very startling words:

> Happy proof! she shall discover
> What joy, what bliss,
> How many heavens at once it is
> To have her God become her Lover.

It would be difficult to be more explicit; but such erotic imagery is by no means uncommon in *Carmen Deo Nostro*. It is not surprising that Santa Teresa of Avila is a favorite subject of Crashaw's: "The Flaming Heart" is perhaps the poet's masterpiece. Santa Teresa herself, who was equally extraordinary as a practical organizer and as a mystic, has left a detailed account of her visions and ecstasies in her *Life*. The most famous of these leaves no doubt that she conceived of the love of God in extremely tangible terms. She saw a beautiful angel holding in his hand a fire-tipped golden arrow, with which again and again he pierced her heart. "The paine of it was so excessive, that it forced me to utter those groanes; and the suavitie, which that extremitie of paine gave, was also so very excessive, that there was no desiring at all, to be ridd of it . . ." [54] This vision needs no Freud to interpret it; and the artists of the sixteenth and seventeenth centuries who depicted it were fully aware of its erotic character, while believing at the same time in its religious significance. The most extraordinary work of baroque sculpture is Bernini's representation of this subject. Santa Teresa and the angel are shown floating on a completely convincing marble cloud; the handsome angel looks at Santa Teresa with an expression of very human love as he prepares to thrust the arrow into her heart; the saint herself is swooning in the last stages of ecstasy. The whole scene takes place in a dramatically lighted and stagelike niche in the Roman church of Santa Maria della Vittoria. To Bernini and his contemporaries, there was nothing inappropriate in so physical an expression of religious feeling; but a skeptical eighteenth-century man of the world, like President de Brosses, apparently unconvinced of the genuineness of such a vision, dismisses this work with a cynical leer. [55]

Many more examples could be cited to show that this note of erotic ecstasy is by no means unusual in baroque art. In another famous piece of sculpture by Bernini, the "Death of the Blessed Ludovica Albertoni," there is the same atmosphere of voluptuous swooning. In Sodoma's "Stigmatization of St.

54. This passage is also extensively reproduced in Warren, *Richard Crashaw*.
55. Cf. C. de Brosses, *Lettres familières sur l'Italie*.

Catherine," [56] Christ hovers tenderly in the sky, while the saint collapses with closed eyes into the arms of two attendant nuns. In Murillo's paintings of St. Anthony with the Christ child, while it would be inexact to describe the atmosphere as erotic, there is nevertheless an extraordinary feeling of physical tenderness; [57] and a similar feeling pervades the same artist's picture of the crucified Christ putting one arm around St. Francis. [58] The general prevalence of such works of art in the late sixteenth and seventeenth centuries suggests that we have here no mere stylistic convention but an actual mode of sensibility; and d'Aubigné, who also represents mystical love in tangible and human forms, shares in that same sensibility.

In the *Préface*, for example, the poet describes his soul as "furieuse de sainct amour," [59] and in *Misères,* calling upon God, he says:

> Puisque de ton amour mon ame est eschauffee,
> Jalouze de ton nom, ma poitrine embrazee
> De ton feu, repurge aussi de mesmes feux
> Le vice naturel de mon cœur vicieuz; [60]

One is reminded here of Donne's

> Take mee to you, imprison mee, for I
> Except you enthrall mee, never shall be free,
> Nor ever chast, except you ravish mee. [61]

Indeed, the *Holy Sonnets* are likewise baroque in feeling. In this one, paradox is combined with the erotic-ecstatic.

The Protestants' prayer which concludes *Misères* contains a wholly human cry for affection and comfort:

> Soyent tes yeux adoucis à guerir nos miseres,
> Ton oreille propice ouverte à nos prieres,
> Ton sein desboutonné à loger nos souspirs, [62]

The passage could serve, incidentally, as an illustration of multiple sense imagery; but we are concerned here with the last line, with d'Aubigné's longing for an unbuttoned bosom to receive his sighs. The poet conceives of a relationship of actual physical tenderness between himself and God.

The frequent use of the verb "pasmer" to express religious ecstasy affords

56. Bernini's statue is in the Church of San Francesco a Ripa, Rome; Sodoma's painting, in the Church of San Domenico, Siena. Both are reproduced by Weisbach.

57. In Seville Cathedral and the Seville Museum.

58. Seville Museum.

59. *Préface,* 132.

60. *Misères,* 45–48.

61. *Holy Sonnets,* XIV, 12–14.

62. *Misères,* 1353–1355.

a close parallel to Bernini's Santa Teresa. In *Princes* the poet invokes Heavenly
Beauty in swooning words:

> Que je sois ta victime, ô celeste beauté,
> Blanche fille du ciel, flambeau d'Eternité!
> Nul bon œil ne la void qui transi ne se pasme,
> Dans cette pasmoison s'esleve au ciel tout ame; [63]

As in baroque sculpture and painting, erotic swooning through the fullness
of religious rapture is regarded as a means of gaining the kingdom of heaven.
In many places in *Les Feux* the déath of martyrs is represented as sensually
ecstatic. Again and again d'Aubigné speaks of the physical sensations of
rapture which they feel in the midst of their torments. I do not mean by this
that the Protestant martyrs are merely described as happy because they are
about to achieve salvation; their actual physical suffering is voluptuous and
death itself an ecstasy. Correggio's picture of the "Martyrdom of Saints
Placidus and Flavia" [64] strikingly exhibits this attitude: at the very moment
when the executioner is plunging his sword into St. Flavia's breasts, she is
gazing upward with an expression of unspeakable delight at the angel who is
bringing her the crown and palm of martyrdom. The following account of
the torture of five Protestants in Lyon makes the experience of martyrdom
seem like a physical joy:

> Au fort de leurs tourmens ils sentirent de l'aise,
> Franchise en leurs liens, du repos en la braise.
> L'amitié dans le feu vous sçeut bien embrazer,
> Vous baisates la mort tous cinq d'un sainct baizer
> Vous baizates la mort: cette mort gracieuse
> Fut de vostre union ardemment amoureuse.[65]

The phraseology is frankly erotic in tone; but there are many other examples
of the same conception of martyrdom. Madame de Graveron, when she is
about to die, exclaims:

> . . . "Je veux jouïr de mes sainctes amours;
> Ces joyaux sont bien peu, l'ame a bien autre gage
> De l'espoux qui lui donne un si haut mariage." [66]

In imagery and moral sensibility, this passage is similar to Crashaw's "Prayer,"
where the gentlewoman's God becomes her lover.

Considering the unabashed sensuality with which d'Aubigné expresses
religious feeling, it is curious to see him denounce Catholics for the very same

63. *Princes*, 175–178.
64. Parma Gallery.
65. *Les Feux*, 457–462.
66. *Les Feux*, 492–494.

practice. The diatribe against the princes of the Valois court attacks the use of profane imagery in religious poetry, classing it as a kind of prostitution:

> Ces levres qui en vain marmottent vos requestes
> Vous les avez ternies en baisers deshonnestes,
> Et ces genous ployez, dessus des licts vilains,
> Prophanes, ont ployé parmi ceux des putains.
> Si depuis quelque temps vos rhymeurs hypocrites,
> Desguisez, ont changé tant de phrases escrites
> Aux prophanes amours, & de mesmes couleurs
> Dont ils servoyent Satan, infames basteleurs,
> Ils colorent encor leurs pompeuses prieres
> De fleurs des vieux payens & fables mensongeres:
> Ces escoliers d'erreur n'ont pas le style apris
> Que l'Esprit de lumiere aprend à nos esprits,
> De quell'oreille Dieu prend les phrases flatresses
> Desquelles ces pipeurs flechissoyent leurs maistresses.[67]

D'Aubigné apparently has a double standard in this matter. It is immoral for a Catholic to address God in the language of human love, and yet *Les Tragiques* is full of such imagery. The truth may be that on this earth intense religious feeling can be expressed in no other way; but whether this is the case or not men of the late sixteenth and seventeenth centuries, both Catholic and Protestant, felt it natural to express their love of God in terms of physical passion. Incarnational art can go no further. It is significant to note the very last line of *Les Tragiques*:

> . . . [l'ame] . . .
> Exstatique se pasme au giron de son Dieu.

67. *Princes*, 425–438.

Chapter IV: PARADOX AND MUTABILITY

1. INTRODUCTION: MONTAIGNE, DONNE, AND SPONDE

Certes, c'est un sujet merveilleusement vain, divers, et ondoyant que l'homme. Il est malaisé d'y fonder jugement constant et uniforme.[1]

Le monde n'est qu'une branloire perenne. Toutes choses y branlent sans cesse: la terre, les rochers du Caucase, les pyramides d'Ægypte, et du branle public et du leur. La constance mesme n'est autre chose qu'un branle plus languissant. . . .[2]

Je ne peints pas l'estre. Je peints le passage.[3]

In these quotations from the *Essais*, Montaigne reveals his belief that reality is neither logically consistent nor static. One is tempted to regard the acute awareness of paradox and mutability in the world, shared by many writers and thinkers of the late sixteenth and seventeenth centuries, as a manifestation of the baroque mind.

In the *Essais* an intense interest in the surprising, the paradoxical and the changeable is everywhere evident. Montaigne loves to emphasize the infinite diversity of the world: not only is each man different from every other man but even single individuals are full of contradictions, varying from one moment to the next. The essays on custom and vanity, as well as the *Apologie de Raymond Sebond*, amass examples of contrasting practices and beliefs. The whole structure of the *Apologie*, indeed, rests on a paradox, for this essay, which begins as a defense of the use of reason in religious matters, soon becomes an attack on reason and a denial of man's ability to know reality.

Furthermore, students of Montaigne have always been struck by the inconsistencies in thought which appear in nearly every essay. It is well known, of course, that these contradictions arise from the author's practice of successive additions to his work: while he constantly interpolates passages, he seldom removes anything. This is because Montaigne is interested in the very evolution of his thought; if he has changed his mind on some subject, the contrast between two opinions held at different times is in itself provocative. In a sense, the evolution of Montaigne's mind is the real subject of the *Essais*. For, as we have just seen, his intention is to describe not static conditions but developments. Montaigne is more concerned with becoming than with being.

1. *Essais*, I, 1.
2. and 3. *Essais*, III, 2.

Aside from this love of contrasts, paradoxes, and contradictions, in addition to his great interest in growth, change, and transformation, Montaigne exhibits in his style an extraordinary concreteness of imagery, comparable to d'Aubigné. To appreciate this characteristic one need only peruse any essay after reading the *Discours de la méthode;* both writers deal with philosophical subjects; yet, while Descartes' prose is abstract and sparing in imagery, Montaigne's has a tangible, picturesque, flesh-and-blood quality. It is for all these reasons that Montaigne, strange as the idea may seem to the traditional student of French literature, may be regarded as a baroque writer. A study of the *Essais* from this point of view would be invaluable; hitherto the question has only been touched upon by Mr. Croll in his study of baroque sentence structure, where it is demonstrated that Montaigne's sentences, instead of presenting in balanced, Ciceronian form the static product of thought, dynamically follow the movements of his mind as he discovers ideas.

However, it is with the baroque interest in paradox and mutability that we are concerned here. Mr. Cleanth Brooks has shown how important a part paradox plays in Donne's poem "The Canonization." There the lovers, who have found a "hermitage" in each other, are contrasted with the world which they have renounced; this renunciation leads to an implied contrast between sacred and profane love; and both of these paradoxes are resolved in the idea that the lovers, by losing the world, have really gained it, so that they have accomplished the same thing as hermit saints.[4] The great appeal which Donne's love poetry has for the present generation springs possibly from the fact that these poems maintain simultaneously the contradictory attitudes of carnal and spiritual love; both body and soul receive their due. The power of this poetry rests upon a psychological tension. We have neither the Platonic love of a Petrarch or a Scève nor Ronsard's frankly Epicurean invitation: "Mignonne, allons voir si la rose . . ." Much of Donne's religious poetry is paradoxical also: for example the sonnet "Batter my heart, three-personed God," which ends with the line, "Nor ever chaste, except you ravish me." "Good Friday Riding Westward" is built upon an antithesis: worldly affairs are taking Donne West, when Good Friday should make him turn his whole being to the East. But with Donne it is not merely states of mind, feelings, and ideas which are contrasted with each other; on a purely technical level, there is constant use of rhetorical devices calculated to arouse surprise: puns, conceits, oxymoron, antithesis, and so on. Thus the whole poetry is permeated with paradox.

For a long time, it was thought that this kind of poetry did not exist in France but Mr. Boase has shown, in a brilliant article entitled "Then Malherbe Came," [5] that certain poets of the end of the sixteenth century, hitherto

4. For the text and an analysis of this poem see Brooks, *The Well-Wrought Urn.*
5. *Criterion* (1930).

obscure, show similar traits of paradox and psychological tension. Stylistic analysis will reveal d'Aubigné to be this kind of poet also; but before examining these features of *Les Tragiques* it will be well to consider for a moment the greatest of the poets mentioned by Mr. Boase: Jean de Sponde. The evolution in modern taste—or perhaps the cyclical recurrence of poetic sensibility— which has brought long-deserved rehabilitation to Donne appears to be rescuing Sponde, for similar reasons, from unmerited oblivion. In recent years, M. Marcel Arland has published a complete edition of Sponde's work,[6] while M. Thierry Maulnier and Mme Dominique Aury have included him in their anthology of baroque poets.[7]

Like Donne Sponde is equally successful in treating two different subjects. Donne is as great in his *Holy Sonnets* and sermons as in his love lyrics; Sponde's poems on death are as fine as his poems on love. In the following sonnet, inner psychological tension has given unusual intensity to the familiar theme of unrequited love:

> Je meurs, et les soucis qui sortent du martyre
> Que me donne l'absence, et les jours, et les nuicts
> Font tant, qu'à tous momens je ne sçay que je suis
> Si j'empire du tout ou bien si je respire.
> Un chagrin survenant mille chagrins m'attire
> En me cuidant aider moy-mesme je me nuis,
> L'infini mouvement de mes roulans ennuis
> M'emporte et je le sens, mais je ne le puis dire.
> Je suis cet Acteon de ces chiens deschiré!
> Et l'esclat de mon ame est si bien alteré
> Qu'elle qui me devroit faire vivre me tuë:
> Deux Deesses nous ont tramé tout nostre sort
> Mais pour divers sujet nous trouvons mesme mort
> Moy de ne la voir point, et luy de l'avoir veuë.

On a very elementary level, it is of course easy to point out the obvious contrasts which exist here. For example, in the second line, days and nights are contrasted; in line 4, "empire" is set off against "respire"; lines 11 and 14 are essentially antitheses: the woman he loves, instead of giving him life, is killing him, and whereas Actaeon dies for having seen Diana, Sponde dies from not seeing his mistress. But more than all this the whole poem is one of inner psychological tension: the implied central paradox is that while the poet is suffering because of the absence of his mistress her presence will make him suffer even more; love, which seems to offer life, in reality leads to death. Two of the images are well worth noting: "Je suis cet Acteon de ces chiens deschiré" is conspicuous for its concrete expression of inner torment; it is no vapid conventional metaphor, blunted by use, but an original and vivid one retaining its

---

6. and 7. Cf. Bibliography. The first two sonnets quoted here are, respectively, V and XVII.

full appeal to the senses. "L'infini mouvement de mes roulans ennuis" is another very remarkable line: not only is it striking and harmonious in itself but it provides another successful example of the translation of a mental state into concrete imagery. Suggestive of the sea, it expresses Sponde's interest in fluid, changing psychological states: like Montaigne, he is here describing not "l'estre" but "le passage." All of these various characteristics—contrast, psychological tension, concreteness of expression, interest in change and fluidity—are elements which, taken together, constitute a strong indication of the baroque style; the presence of one of them would not be specially significant, but their conjunction makes it permissible to term Sponde baroque.

Let us take another example from Sponde's love sonnets. This one also is remarkable for its revelation of a divided soul:

> Je sens dedans mon ame une guerre civile
> D'un parti ma raison, mes sens d'autre parti,
> Dont le bruslant discord ne peut estre amorti
> Tant chacun son tranchant l'un contre l'autre affile.
> Mais mes sens sont armez d'un verre si fragile
> Que si le cœur bien tost ne s'en est departi
> Tout l'heur vers ma raison se verra converti,
> Comme au parti plus fort plus juste et plus utile,
> Mes sens veulent ployer sous ce pesant fardeau
> Des ardeurs que me donne un esloigné flambeau,
> Au rebours la raison me renforce au martyre.
> Faisons comme dans Rome, à ce peuple mutin
> De mes sens inconstans arrachons-les en fin
> Et que nostre raison y plante son Empire.

This sonnet, like the last one, as the phrase "esloigné flambeau" indicates, is inspired by the absence of Sponde's mistress. It deals fundamentally with a conflict between reason and passion; and though in the end reason is allowed to triumph, we feel that this triumph is an insecure and impermanent one. In fact, in the second quatrain, the poet seems to dread the ascendancy of reason, as if this were an enemy victory; and in line 11 he speaks of the martyrdom which reason is inflicting upon him. So actually the poem maintains two conflicting attitudes throughout. It is interesting, incidentally, to consider the civil war image in this sonnet along with the Actaeon metaphor in the first one; as early as 1914 the Norwegian scholar Vedel suggested that hunting and war images, used to express psychological states, were a characteristic of the baroque style in poetry.[8]

Sponde's finest poems are probably his *Stances de la Mort* and his twelve sonnets on the same subject. Here again we have the poetry of paradox, for

8. Vedel, "Den digteriske Barokstil omkring aar 1600."

Sponde is unable to choose between life and death. On the one hand, the joys of this world are very dear to him; on the other, he feels that ultimate peace and happiness can be gained only through death. And so the *Stances* are full of lines like

> Faisons, faisons naufrage, et jettons nous au port [9]

which in their antithesis are expressive of a very great psychological tension.

Sonnet II of the "Autres Sonnets sur le mesme sujet par le dit sieur de Sponde" contains a skillful interweaving of the themes of life and death:

> Mais si faut-il mourir, et la vie orgueilleuse
> Qui brave de la mort, sentira ses fureurs,
> Les soleils haleront ces journalieres fleurs,
> Et le temps crevera ceste ampoule venteuse.
> Ce beau flambeau qui lance une flamme fumeuse,
> Sur le verd de la cire esteindra ses ardeurs,
> L'huile de ce tableau ternira ses couleurs,
> Et ses flots se rompront à la rive escumeuse.
> J'ay veu ces clairs esclairs passer devant mes yeux,
> Et le tonnerre encor qui gronde dans les Cieux
> Où d'une ou d'autre part esclatera l'orage,
> J'ay veu fondre la neige et ses torrens tarir,
> Ces lyons rugissans je les ay veus sans rage,
> Vivez, hommes, vivez, mais si faut-il mourir.

In a sense, this sonnet contains within its small compass the two attitudes toward death which Montaigne exhibits in different periods of his life. Is true wisdom a learning how to die (*Que philosopher c'est apprendre à mourir*), or is the wisest course to do as the peasants in the essay *De la Physionomie,* who accept life and death from the hands of nature without thinking about them? The poem begins with an assertion of the inevitability of death and the transitoriness of earthly beauties; yet in the very enumeration of the fragile marvels of nature Sponde is gradually won over by the love of life. The first hemistich of the last line calls upon men to make the most of life; and then, suddenly at the end, the original theme of the inevitability of death returns. The effect produced by the final hemistich is similar to Marvell's:

> But at my back I alwaies hear
> Time's wingéd chariot hurrying near.

(Indeed, "To His Coy Mistress" contains a typically baroque fusion of the contrasting themes of love and death.) Thus Sponde's sonnet affirms simultaneously the vanity and the value of life. But no less remarkable than this

9. L. 114.

conflict of themes is the painting of what Montaigne calls "le passage." There is a sense of the fluidity of nature, of the constant transformation of all earthly things; like Montaigne, Sponde is acutely interested in becoming rather than being. Nearly all the images in this sonnet express change, metamorphosis, or degeneration. The flowers fade, the torch goes out, the painting loses its colors, the snow melts, the torrents dry up, the lions cease their roaring. Although these are changes in the outer world, they are symbolic changes and thus reveal an affinity with Montaigne's interest in psychological becoming. The sonnet as a whole is a fine illustration of the poetry of paradox and mutability.

Before turning to the analysis of these same elements in the poetry of d'Aubigné, it may be helpful to consider a final example from Sponde's sonnets on death. This one is No. XII; and though there are others of greater poetic merit (for instance, V: "Helas, contez vos jours," and IX: "Qui sont, qui sont ceux là, dont le cœur idolatre) the evenly balanced antithesis of its form is an effective illustration of the poet's inner conflict.

> Tout s'enfle contre moy, tout m'assaut, tout me tente,
> Et le monde, et la chair, et l'Ange revolté,
> Dont l'onde, dont l'effort, dont le charme inventé
> Et m'abisme, Seigneur, et m'esbranle, et m'enchante.
> Quelle nef, quel appuy, quelle oreille dormante,
> Sans peril, sans tomber, et sans estre enchanté,
> Me donras-tu ton Temple où vit ta Sainteté,
> Ton invincible main, et ta voix si constante?
> Et quoy? mon Dieu, je sens combattre maintesfois,
> Encore avec ton Temple, et ta main, et ta voix,
> Cest Ange revolté, ceste chair, et ce Monde.
> Mais ton Temple pourtant, ta main, ta voix sera
> La nef, l'appuy, l'oreille, où ce charme perdra,
> Où mourra cest effort, où se perdra ceste onde.

The images in this sonnet appear in groups of three which are contrasted with each other: on the one hand, the world, the flesh, and the devil; on the other hand, the temple, the voice, and the hand of God. Similarly, the "onde," the "effort," and the "charme inventé" are set off against the "nef," the "appuy," and the "oreille dormante." The curious twisting given to the echo device should also be observed: line 11 repeats, in reverse order, the world, the flesh, and the rebellious angel of line 2; lines 13 and 14 reverse the images of line 3. This procedure increases the already extraordinary symmetry of the poem, and this very symmetry emphasizes the unresolved conflict in the poet's mind. As a Christian Sponde believes in God; but as a man he still loves the world. The attractions of this world are expressed by images of motion and fluidity (note the verbs "enfler," "abîmer," "ébranler," and the symbol of the sea), whereas God is rendered by images of firmness and solidity: a hand, a support, a ship, a temple. Flux and change are contrasted with stability and repose.

It is hoped that these illustrations from Sponde will serve to explain what is meant by the poetry of paradox and mutability, and thus make clearer the same characteristics in *Les Tragiques*. This aspect of d'Aubigné's style, it will be seen, reveals itself both in form and in content: in form, by the use of such rhetorical devices as oxymoron, conceits, contrasts, and metaphoric antithesis; in content, by the poet's interest in psychological tension, disguise, and metamorphosis.

2. OXYMORON

Of all rhetorical devices oxymoron is perhaps the one which exhibits contrast in most compact form. It frequently consists only of a noun modified by a contradictory adjective, and so within the compass of just two words expresses that sense of antithesis which, as we have seen, is so congenial to the baroque mind. For these reasons it seems appropriate to consider it first. *Les Tragiques* offers many specimens.

Préface, 311–312.

> Il y a de la peine oisive
> Et du loisir qui est labeur.

Here the two cases of oxymoron are further contrasted with each other; they are linked by the approximate echo "oisive"–"loisir," and the second of the two is emphasized by alliteration.

Misères, 505. Description of the mother turned cannibal by hunger, who devours her own child.

> La mere . . . pitoyable & farouche,

Such a situation interests d'Aubigné because it permits him to indulge his well-known predilection for horrifying the reader, but it is also a situation of inner conflict, since the mother struggles between hunger and love. The juxtaposition of the words "pitoyable" and "farouche" expresses this clash of emotions.

Misères, 613. The poet is addressing France and speaking of the calamities of civil war.

> Que si tu vis encor, c'est la mourante vie

Misères, 1273. Beginning of the prayer to God:

> Tu vois, juste vengeur, les fleaux de ton Eglise,

Misères, 1289. From the same prayer:

> Chastie en ta douceur, . . .

Princes, 963. The hypocritical flatterers who poison the king's mind.

> L'arsenic ensucré de leurs belles paroles,

Les Feux, 890. The heroic reply of Etienne Brun, a Protestant martyr from Dauphiné, when he heard his sentence of execution.

> Respondit qu'on l'avoit condamné à la vie.

Les Feux, 988.

> Mais les martyrs ont eu moins de contentement
> De qui la laide nuict cache le beau tourment:

Les Fers, 734. A line from an elaborate metaphor, comparing the Church to a field of trampled grain; only the ears of wheat nestling amid the hawthorn have escaped.

> Des tuteurs aubepins rudement caressees,

Vengeances, 66.

> Ces fermes visions, ces veritables songes;

Vengeances, 657. Epithet applied to Julian the Apostate and his pagan philosophers, who murder the soul:

> Pacifiques meurtriers, . . .

Vengeances, 703.

> O martyres aimez! ô douce affliction!

Jugement, 18. The will of God:

> Estre craint par amour & non aimé par crainte;

As in the first example, two cases of oxymoron are placed in antithesis.

As we look over these expressions—dying life, just avenger, sugared arsenic, compassionate and fierce, condemned to life, beautiful torment, sweet affliction —I think we feel that they are more than a mere literary device, dictated by a passing fashion. As a matter of fact, *Les Tragiques,* far more than the poetry of the Pléiade, is drawn from direct experience of life rather than from literary models; this is true despite the manifestly biblical inspiration of many lines. The poet who, through natural inclination, chooses such means of expression as the above is acutely aware of the paradoxes of life. Some minds are so constituted that they always endeavor to reduce reality to a logical consistency, and believe that the world can be explained by a unified system; others, however, see contrasts, contradictions, and variety everywhere. It is evident that Montaigne's mind was of the second type; but so also, despite his constant struggle to find unity through religious faith, was Agrippa d'Aubigné's.

However, oxymoron is significant in another respect: its artistic purpose is to surprise the reader. D'Aubigné is especially fond of those literary effects which are attained through surprise. Like all verbal magicians from Rabelais to James Joyce, he enjoys playing with words and confronting us with unexpected conclusions. One way of renewing the magic of language is to jolt the reader by using puns and conceits in unusual connections.

3. PUNS AND CONCEITS

> . . . If he do bleed
> I'll gild the faces of the grooms withal,
> For it must seem their guilt.

This gruesome pun, made by Lady Macbeth immediately after the murder of Duncan, is representative of the sensibility of another age. What seems especially strange to modern taste is the use of a pun in a tragic situation; yet this is by no means the only example to be found in Shakespeare, and *Les Tragiques* abounds in conceits of a similar nature. In some cases there are actual puns; but frequently also there is merely the playful juxtaposition of words different in meaning and similar, though not identical, in sound.

In *La Chambre dorée* the poet mentions a famous session of the Parlement of Paris, held in June, 1559, when, in the presence of the king, the Catholic orthodoxy of all counselors was investigated; this inquisition was called *la Mercuriale*. The event, for d'Aubigné, is basically a serious and tragic one; nevertheless he does not hesitate to exploit the verbal possibilities of the name:

> De là se peut la Cour, en se faisant esgalle
> A Mercure maqreau, dire Mercurialle.[10]

Again, *Les Feux*, that honor roll of heroic martyrs, is in no sense meant to be a humorous book. Yet conceits are present here too. The poet tells us of the martyrdom of an Englishman named Thomas Haux, who was burned at the stake in 1555 for having professed heretical opinions on the subject of baptism. The episode is introduced by the age-old pun, which goes back to Latin times, about Angles and angels:

> Poursuivons les Anglois qui de succez estranges
> Ont fait nommer leur terre à bon droict terre d'Anges.[11]

10. *La Chambre dorée,* 521–522.
11. *Les Feux,* 125–126.

In another passage from the English part of his martyrology, d'Aubigné lists three young women who were put to death for heresy in the reign of Edward VI: Agnes Fauster, Agnes Snode, and Agnes George. Their names give him an opportunity to exclaim:

> Trois Agnez, trois agneaux! [12]

Among other victims of *Les Feux* is Giovanni di Montalcino, a former Franciscan friar who was thrown into prison for preaching heretical sermons, then strangled and burned in Rome in 1553. According to the poet, this martyr's last sermon, delivered at the stake just before the fire was lighted, consisted essentially of a fifty-line conceit upon the words "seul," "seule," and "seulement." By playing with the meanings of these three words, Montalcino is able to make a brief résumé of the main differences between Protestant and Catholic doctrine:

> "Trois mots feront par tout le vray departement
> Des contraires raisons: *seul, seule,* & *seulement.*" [13]

To the twentieth-century reader it seems incongruous indeed that a man should resort to a form of punning when expressing his religious convictions at the point of death; or, more accurately, since after all d'Aubigné is responsible for this speech, that a serious poet should seize such an occasion for a display of verbal virtuosity.

The last words of Etienne Brun (the child-martyr from Dauphiné) contain a pun also. Though accepting with silent stoicism his own sentence of death, the young boy breaks down when he sees his father and uncle tied to the stake; bitterly reproved for his show of weakness, he recovers himself, explaining that though the instincts of his flesh and blood make him tremble at the sight, his soul is unmoved:

> Mon amour est esmeu, l'ame n'est pas esmeuë;
> Le sang, non pas le sens, se trouble à vostre veuë; [14]

The pun on "sang" and "sens" is of course obvious, but to be noted also is the conceit based on the similarity of the words "amour" and "ame."

D'Aubigné, who had but little love for the papacy, singles out for special admiration a Capuchin monk who called Clement VIII Antichrist to his face:

> De mesme escole vint, après un peu d'espace,
> Le maigre Capucin: cettui-ci, en la face
> Du Pape non Clement, l'appela Antechrist, [15]

12. *Les Feux*, 325.
13. *Les Feux*, 655–656.
14. *Les Feux*, 937–938.
15. *Les Feux*, 1205–1207.

The play on the pope's name does not display any great degree of originality, but it may be supposed to have given pleasure to the poet's partisan heart.

It will be remembered that *Les Fers* contains an account not only of the Massacre of St. Bartholomew in Paris, but also of all the other massacres which took place throughout the provinces at the same time. Two of the provincial cities where Protestants were slaughtered provide opportunities for puns:

> Et toy, Sens, insensé, tu appris à la Seine
> Premier à s'engraisser de substance humaine,[16]

and

> Lyon, tous tes lions refuserent l'office: [17]

To d'Aubigné, these massacres were no laughing matter and his intention here is certainly not to make a joke out of persecutions. Rather, he wishes to shock the reader into attention by the startling use of a word. Likewise, there is no desire to ridicule the Protestant leader Coligny in the epithet "Amiral admirable." [18] The poet is fascinated by the simple idea that words of similar sound can have contrasting meanings, or meanings that are unexpectedly appropriate.

We find the "sens-sang" pun again in *Vengeances*. The most horrible of Nero's crimes is described in a passage full of conceits:

> Tu ne fus pas Romain envers ta belle Rome;
> D'où l'ame tu receus, l'ame tu fis sortir:
> Si ton sens ne sentoit, le sang devoit sentir.[19]

(In case the reader has had difficulty in deciphering these lines, it should be explained that, according to tradition, Nero had his mother killed and her body opened up through a perverted curiosity to see the actual womb from which he was born.)

Other conceits in the sixth book, based like the Pope Clement pun on proper names, include:

> Constant, par trop constant à suivre la doctrine
> D'Arius . . .[20]

and

> Quand le comte Felix (nom sans felicité),[21]

The punishment visited by God upon the persecutors of the Waldensian Protestants gives rise to one of d'Aubigné's most egregious puns. These in-

16. *Les Fers*, 585–586.
17. *Les Fers*, 1073.
18. Cf. *Les Fers*, 693.
19. *Vengeances*, 530–532.
20. *Vengeances*, 673.
21. *Vengeances*, 795.

quisitors were attacked by a mysterious disease in which worms gradually
devoured their bodies. The poet hopes that God will inflict similar vengeance
on Philip II for his part in the Spanish Inquisition, and that *Les Tragiques*
will render the name of the king forever infamous. This desire is expressed by
a play on the double sense of the word "vers":

> O Roy, mespris du ciel, terreur de l'univers,
> Herode glorieux, n'attens rien que des vers.
> Espagnol triomphant, Dieu vengeur à sa gloire
> Peindra de vers ton corps, de mes vers ta memoire.[22]

The striking thing about the majority of these conceits is that they occur in
the midst of passages on death or martyrdom; and though they were clearly
not felt to be vulgar or inappropriate, their presence does reveal an admiration
for virtuosity and a love of surprise.

4. METAPHORIC ANTITHESIS

The rhetorical figure known as syllepsis is defined as follows by the *Oxford
English Dictionary:* "A figure by which a word . . . is made to refer to two
or more other words in the same sentence, while properly applying to or agree-
ing with only one of them, or applying in different senses (e.g., literal and
metaphorical)." Syllepsis, in this latter sense of contrasting the literal and
figurative meanings of a word, is a device often encountered in the poetry of
the late sixteenth and seventeenth centuries. The phenomenon has been observed by Mr. Hatzfeld, in his article on the French religious lyric of the seventeenth century: he gives one form of it the name of *Schleierantithese,* or veiled
antithesis.[23] In this type of conceit the poet begins by misleading the reader
into accepting a single meaning for the sylleptic word; then the second meaning is suddenly "unveiled," producing an effect of surprise and contrast.

We often understand the essence of a stylistic peculiarity best by looking
at an extreme or silly specimen. And so we cannot, I think, do better than
follow Mr. Hatzfeld's example and look at Trissotin's sonnet in *Les Femmes
savantes.* Here we soon come upon the lines:

> Quoi! sans respecter votre rang
> Elle se prend à votre sang,

The reader is naturally induced to believe that the word "sang" is being used
in the sense of "aristocratic rank"; the sonnet is, however, a sort of riddle and
he eventually discovers that the subject really is Princess Uranie's fever; so
"sang" should have been interpreted in its literal meaning all along.

22. *Vengeances,* 863–866.
23. Cf. Hatzfeld, "Der Barockstil der religiösen klassischen Lyrik in Frankreich."

This form of antithesis is of frequent occurrence in *Les Tragiques.* Luckily, most of the examples are not so ridiculous as Molière's specimen, and they do not all conform rigidly to this pattern. Since syllepsis often signifies a grammatical as well as a rhetorical tour de force, and since veiled antithesis suggests that some delay occurs between the moment of deception and the surprising revelation, it seems more appropriate, in the case of *Les Tragiques,* to speak of *metaphoric antithesis.* For purposes of surprise and contrast, d'Aubigné is prone to exploit this difference between literal and figurative meanings within the limited compass of a single line or short passage.

The story of the cannibalistic mother, described as simultaneously "compassionate and ferocious," has already figured in our discussions of horror and of oxymoron. But two lines of the passage deserve reexamination here:

La mere deffaisant, pitoyable et farouche,
Les liens de pitié avec ceux de sa couche,[24]

The word "liens" is first used in a purely metaphórical sense—the *ties* of pity. But in the second hemistich it has a literal meaning—the strings or ribbons which tie the child in its cradle. The reader has to shift his interpretation in the middle of the line, being jolted from the language of imagery to that of straightforward expression. And so we have that specialized form of contrast, in some ways analogous to the pun, called metaphoric antithesis. When the mother actually begins to devour her baby, the poet says

Elle ouvre le passage au sang et aux esprits; [25]

In this case the literal meaning comes first and the metaphor afterwards.

One long section of *Misères* attacks the practice of dueling. D'Aubigné sums up the moral dilemma in which a Christian man of honor finds himself when forced, by the corrupt customs of the Valois court, to fight a duel:

. . . la pestifere loy
Reduisant d'un bon cœur la valeur prisonniere
A voir devant l'espee, & l'enfer par derriere.[26]

Antithesis is present here both in content and in form. The fundamental idea expressed is the psychological tension resulting from a conflict in duties; considered syntactically, the verb "voir" has both a literal and a figurative direct object. (With regard to this question of a conflict in duties, it may not be inappropriate to suggest here that the opposition between two different conceptions of honor, as seen in *Le Cid,* is baroque in theme and expression:

24. *Misères,* 505–506.
25. *Misères,* 539.
26. *Misères,* 1066.

> Tu t'es, en m'offensant, montré digne de moi;
> Je me dois, par ta mort, montrer digne de toi.)²⁷ [27]

The description of the Paris law courts, in Book III of *Les Tragiques,* also contains a verbal shift:

> Encor falut-il voir cette Chambre Doree,
> De justice jadis, d'or maintenant paree [28]

The verb "paree" is used in two different senses. Hardly has the abstract concept of justice been presented to us when, in a sudden comedown, we are confronted by the concrete image of gold. Since we do not expect the change in meaning, the bathos of "or" hits us with particular force.

The Protestant martyrs of *Les Feux* are described as

> Armez de la priere & non point des couteaux.[29]

Here again the sudden and surprising descent from the figurative to the literal gives a brutal power to the word "couteaux."

In the account of the imprisonment of another martyr, Richard de Gastine, the metaphoric antithesis undergoes considerable elaboration:

> Dans l'obscure prison, par les claires raisons
> Il vainquit l'obstiné, redressa le debile;
> Asseuré de sa mort il prescha l'Evangile.
> L'escole de lumiere, en cette obscurité,
> Donnoit aux enferrés l'entiere liberté.
> Son ame, de l'enfer au paradis ravie,
> Aux ombres de la mort eut la voix de la vie.[30]

The point here is not that light and darkness, or life and death are contrasted; such antitheses are so common in poetry as to offer no special interest. Of greater significance is the fact that darkness and death have throughout a perfectly straightforward physical meaning, whereas light and life have a symbolical, religious meaning. The constant shifting back and forth from one level to the other gives this passage its peculiar character.

Very similar stylistically is d'Aubigné's apostrophe to the martyrs:

> O cœurs mourans à vie, indomptés & vainqueurs,
> O combien vostre mort fit revivre de cœurs! [31]

Though these men have, in a literal sense, been put to death, nevertheless, symbolically and religiously, they are unconquered; and the physical fact of

27. *Le Cid,* 931–932.
28. *La Chambre dorée,* 234–235.
29. *Les Feux,* 712.
30. *Les Feux,* 724–730.
31. *Les Feux,* 975–976.

their death is contrasted with the metaphorical rebirth of those who, upon witnessing their martyrdom, have been converted to Protestantism.

The book of *Vengeances* contains a rogues' gallery of Roman emperors punished by God for their misdeeds. One of them is Valerian, who had been hostile to the Christians and was finally taken prisoner by the Persian king Sapor. According to tradition, Sapor killed Valerian by skinning him alive. The fate of the Roman emperor is commemorated by d'Aubigné in the following metaphoric antithesis:

> Plus lui devoit peser sang sur sang, mal sur mal,
> Que ce Roy sur son dos qui montoit à cheval,
> Qui en fin l'escorcha vif, le despouïllant, comme
> Vif il fut despouïllé des sentimens de l'homme.[32]

Here the words "peser" and "despouïller" have their literal and figurative meanings contrasted.

The death of Arius, the author of the Arian heresy, was, d'Aubigné informs us, also an effect of the wrath of God. As retribution for spreading false doctrine, he was suddenly taken ill and

> . . . versa en une orde latrine
> Ventre & vie à la fois: . . .[33]

The scene is, incidentally, a good example of the horrifying realism of *Les Tragiques;* and it may be further observed that the metaphoric antithesis is further embellished by a triple alliteration.

Coming to more modern times, the poet castigates Charles IX and his brother the Duke of Anjou, the former for his responsibility for the Massacre of St. Bartholomew, the latter for a bloody and abortive attack on the city of Antwerp. Both of them later died of hemoptysis (a spitting of blood) and d'Aubigné sees in this a suitable divine punishment:

> Leur rouge mort aussi fut marque de leur vie,
> Leur puante charongne & l'ame empuantie
> Partagerent, sortans de l'impudique flanc,
> Une mer de forfaicts & un fleuve de sang.[34]

In one case the stink is actual, in the other metaphorical; and whereas the sea is figurative, the river, with all due allowance for hyperbole, is literal.

Of another group of punished sinners in *Vengeances* the poet remarks

> En attendant le feu préparé pour leurs ames
> Ces enflammés au corps ont ressenti des flammes.[35]

32. *Vengeances*, 595–598.
33. *Vengeances*, 674–675.
34. *Vengeances*, 809–812.
35. *Vengeances*, 869–870.

It may be objected that in this illustration, as in some others quoted here, there is no true metaphoric antithesis, since for d'Aubigné the flames of hell were probably not symbolic but real. Nevertheless, even if this is not, strictly speaking, a contrast between the actual and the metaphoric, the fundamental meanings are not the same, for this world is being contrasted with the next. The physical tortures of the body are an anticipation of the spiritual tortures of the soul. The shift in sense creates surprise.

5. The Surprise Climax

According to Marino in the preface to *Adone*, no man should attempt to be a poet unless he is capable of amazing his readers. The main purpose of poetry is to cause astonishment; and to this end no metaphor is too far-fetched, no conceit too fantastic. The devices studied so far in this chapter depend for their effect, to a great extent, upon surprise. It is the element of unexpectedness in oxymoron, pun, and metaphoric antithesis which captures the reader's attention. As such, Marino would have approved of all of them. Mr. Hatzfeld feels that even more than antithesis devices which arouse surprise are characteristic of baroque poetry.[36] To one of these devices he has given the name of *Schlussblitz;* this may be freely though conveniently translated as the surprise climax. D'Aubigné is very fond of such surprise climaxes: a frequent technique in *Les Tragiques* is to crown a lengthy oratorical development with a brief, violent, unexpected statement. These "punch lines," as we shall see, may derive their effect from any of a number of causes: brutality or irony of tone, simple words following elaborate language, or just unexpectedness. The procedure is in reality a part of d'Aubigné's horror technique; but here we are chiefly concerned with the element of surprise.

The invective against Catherine de' Medici in *Misères* provides several illustrations. D'Aubigné first begins his diatribe on line 699:

> Cet enfer nourrissoit en ses obscuritez
> Deux esprits . . .

As he enumerates the crimes perpetrated by the queen mother, his indignation keeps mounting in violence. Catherine is repeatedly called Jezebel, blamed for all the miseries of France and, in a startling image, made directly responsible for the death of five hundred thousand soldiers:

> Cinq cens mille soldats n'eussent crevé, poudreux
> Sur le champ maternel . . .

After ninety lines of violent denunciation, the poet pauses to catch his breath; but the mighty build-up is climaxed with the following venomous couplet:

36. *Op. cit.*

> Tu n'as ta soif de sang qu'à demi arrosee,
> Ainsi que d'un peu d'eau la flamme est embrasee.

After the vicious picture of the queen inciting civil war, the reader does not see how anything more ferocious in tone can follow; yet this couplet, breathing an even more intense hatred than the preceding ninety lines, comes as an unexpected shock. We then have a comparatively quiet passage, describing the sadistic little games which Catherine used to play as a child in the convent in Florence. Underneath the calm surface, however, the poet's resentment is seething; it suddenly erupts in another Schlussblitz:

> Or ne veuille le ciel avoir jugé la France
> A servir septante ans de gibier à Florence!

A further recital of the queen's crimes brings us to another brutal climax:

> Et les feux de Neron ne furent point des feux
> Pres de ceux que vomit ce serpent monstrueux.

At times, the shock comes from bitter irony:

> . . . cette maison n'est que la maison de France,
> La maison qu'elle sappe . . .

The accumulation of scenes of violence in *Les Tragiques* has already been discussed; the point to be stressed here is that even in the midst of several hundred lines of steady hatred and horror, the poet still finds stylistic means of shocking the reader anew. We think, as horror is added to horror, that we have become inured to all emotions of surprise—and then we are surprised by some punch line which momentarily interrupts the steady flow of mounting passion.

D'Aubigné's attack upon the practice of dueling can serve as a further illustration of his technique of surprise. Here, the long and impassioned crescendo is abruptly broken by four simple words:

> On appelle aujourd'hui n'avoir rien fait qui vaille
> D'avoir percé premier l'espais d'une bataille,
> D'avoir premier porté une enseigne au plus haut
> Et franchi devant tous la breche par assaut.
> Se jetter contre espoir dans la ville assiegee,
> La sauver demi-prise & rendre encouragee,
> Fortifier, camper ou se loger parmi
> Les gardes, les efforts d'un puissant ennemi,
> Employer, sans manquer de cœur ni de cervelle,
> L'espee d'une main, de l'autre la truelle,
> Bien faire une retraitte, ou d'un scadron battu
> R'allier les deffaicts, cela n'est plus vertu.

> La voici pour ce temps: bien prendre une querelle
> Pour un oiseau ou chien, pour garce ou maquerelle,
> Au plaisir d'un vallet, d'un bouffon gazouïllant
> Qui veut, dit-il, sçavoir si son maistre est vaillant.[37]

For eleven and a half lines d'Aubigné stirs us with scenes of battle and heroism, truly remarkable for their vigor of movement; then he pulls us up sharply with the words "cela n'est plus vertu." It is not only that these words interrupt the epic movement of the preceding lines and thereby shock the reader into a heightened alertness, but also the very brusqueness of the expression contrasts sharply with the heroic language of the battle descriptions. The four lines which describe the mock-heroic deeds of the duelists also gain their effect through contrast and surprise. The epic tone unexpectedly gives way to irony; we receive a jolt of bathos as we pass from the dust of battle to the intrigues of the boudoir. In this case, actually it is a surprise anticlimax rather than a surprise climax.

The more usual method, however, is to cause astonishment by an increase rather than by a decrease of fury. Such is the case when the poet passes from the description of the tyrannies and gladiatorial combats of Nero's reign to the recital of the crimes of the pope. The portrait of Nero is concluded with the words:

> "J'esclave les plus grands: mon plaisir pour tous droicts
> Donne aux gueux la couronne & le bissac aux Rois." [38]

One might expect this to be the climax of the development, but d'Aubigné has reserved a surprise for us. The language of the pope is even more brutally cynical:

> Cet ancien loup romain n'en sçeut pas davantage;
> Mais le loup de ce siecle a bien autre langage:
> "Je dispense, dit-il, du droict contre le droict;
> Celui que j'ai damné, quand le ciel le voudroit,
> Ne peut estre sauvé; . . ."

It is often a characteristic of d'Aubigné's poetry that, just when all possible horrors seem to have been exhausted, we rise to another and unexpected climax. The poet appears to be telling us continually that the world is still more strange and terrible than we think it is.

If a climax is to be a real climax, it must not be allowed to drag on too long; that is why in most cases the Schlussblitz consists at most of a line or two, and generally possesses a certain compact, epigrammatic quality. In *Princes*

---

37. *Misères*, 1121–1136.
38. *Misères*, 1231–1232.

d'Aubigné imagines that a king, weary of lies and flattery, has decided to wander incognito among his subjects in order to find out what they really think of him. Discovering the truth and realizing in what a fool's paradise he has been living, he feels that his only chance of happiness is to keep the disguise permanently. But these idealistic musings are short-lived; with a shock, reality returns:

> Mais estant en sa cour, des masquereaux la troupe
> Luy faict humer le vice en l'obscur d'une coupe.[39]

Perhaps the most tersely ironic use of the punch line occurs when the virtuous young man visits the court of the Valois. There he sees some people who are obviously very influential, and in his innocence he inquires who they are:

> "Ont-ils sur l'Espagnol conquis quelque province?
> Ont-ils par leurs conseils relevé un malheur?
> Delivré leurs pays par extreme valeur?
> Ont-ils sauvé le Roy, commandé quelque armee,
> Et par elle gaigné quelque heureuse journee?"
> A tout fut respondu: "Mon jeune homme, je croy
> Que vous estes bien neuf, ce sont mignons du Roy." [40]

The structure of this passage is analogous to that of the attack on dueling: an oratorical development is arrested by an ironic epigram. The technique of concealing the true identity of the "mignons" until the end, and then revealing it at the climax, is likewise employed in the descriptions of some of the vices that inhabit the *Chambre dorée*. The allegories of Hypocrisy, Inconstancy, Stupidity, Cruelty, Clownishness, and Legal Formalism are treated in this manner. Each character is described at some length and its identity suddenly unveiled in the final line. The orators at American political conventions would be puzzled to hear that they employ a baroque technique in introducing candidates, but actually many of their speeches are constructed on this model, with a name dramatically disclosed at the end.

One final illustration of this device should be sufficient. This is from *Les Fers*. D'Aubigné is deploring the fact that Paris should be the city to be disgraced by such a crime against humanity as the Massacre of St. Bartholomew. So he begins by evoking the former glories of Paris and when the mood has been created abruptly shatters it by contrasting the horrors of the present:

> La cité où jadis la loy fut reveree,
> Qui à cause des loix fut jadis honoree,
> Qui dispensoit en France & la vie & les droicts,

39. *Princes*, 365–366.
40. *Princes*, 1166–1172.

Où fleurissoyent les arts, la mere de nos Rois,
Vid et souffrit en soy la populace armee
Trepigner la justice, à ses pieds diffamee.[41]

The kind of mind that delights in surprises is the mind that is interested in the complexity and diversity of the world; and so a study of the surprise climax takes its proper place in any consideration of the poetry of paradox and mutability. Although the use of oxymoron, conceits, metaphoric antithesis, or surprise climax may appear to be a superficial manifestation of rhetoric, a passing vogue of style, actually it corresponds to the writer's fundamental conception of reality. For form can never be wholly separated from content, and there is such a thing as the baroque mind as well as baroque rhetoric. Those writers who, like Descartes and the seventeenth-century classicists, believe that all reality can be explained in terms of a unified system are unlikely to take pleasure in devices depending on surprise, since surprises are a violation of the logical unity which such men are seeking to establish. The degeneration of the ideal of the *honnête homme,* after two centuries of classicism, into a frozen intellectual apathy is ably satirized in Stendhal's portrait of Madame de la Mole, who above all else had a horror of being surprised: "L'*imprévu* produit par la sensibilité est l'horreur des grandes dames; c'est l'antipode des convenances." [42] But to d'Aubigné (despite his apparent singlemindedness of religious faith), as to Sponde and Montaigne, the world is not static; it is "divers et ondoyant." And since this very diversity is the spice of life, surprise is not a humiliating emotion; having renounced the pretension of being able to explain everything, such minds are free to enjoy contrasts and paradoxes. The attitude of d'Aubigné and other baroque writers is not "nil admirari," but rather "omnia admirari."

6. CONTRAST

The rhetorical figures hitherto considered are, as has been observed, merely detailed aspects of a broader question: d'Aubigné's tendency to visualize the world as "divers et ondoyant" and hence to delight in contrasts. I do not maintain that the use of antithesis characterizes an author as baroque: poets of all ages have, of course, employed this figure of speech—and no one, perhaps, to greater excess than Victor Hugo. It would be more reasonable to reverse the proposition and to say that all baroque writers love contrast. If we find an author of the period 1575–1630 approximately, who, in addition to expressing himself in antitheses, uses richly concrete imagery, creates theatrical scenes, employs the "merveilleux chrétien," and is inspired by a strong moral purpose,

41. *Les Fers,* 793–798.
42. *Le Rouge et le noir,* chap. 35.

we are justified in terming him baroque. It is the conjunction of all these phenomena, rather than any one taken by itself, which is conclusive.

In any case, contrast is a conspicuous feature of *Les Tragiques* and must be considered in any study of the style of this poem. Up to this point we have been dealing with specialized forms of contrast; now for a moment let us look at contrast in its broadest sense. Antithesis is so frequent throughout *Les Tragiques* that the examples will have to be limited to a few representative specimens.

Préface, 233:

> Là les agnelets de l'Eglise
> Sautent au nez du loup romain.

Préface, 304:

> Pour, dans les feux d'un chaud esté
> Boire la glace à la fontaine,

Préface, 373:

> Vous louerez Dieu, ils trembleront;
> Vous chanterez, ils pleureront:

Misères, 233:

> Le sage justicier est traîné au supplice,
> Le mal-faicteur luy faict son procès; l'injustice
> Est principe de droict; . . .

In *Misères,* 563–592, there are two sharply contrasting scenes of pageantry: the entry of the good old king and of the modern tyrant into a French city. The scenes in themselves are dramatic and full of visual appeal, but they gain their chief effectiveness by being set off against each other.

Misères, 733. Remarks on the regency of Catherine de' Medici:

> Le diadème sainct sur la teste insolente,
> Le sacré sceptre au poing d'une femme impuissante,

Misères, 1189. The deaths of a martyr and of a sinner are contrasted:

> Des triomphans martyrs la façon n'est pas telle:
> Le premier martyr de la haute querelle
> Prioit pour ses meurtriers & voyoit en priant
> Sa place au ciel ouvert, son Christ l'y conviant.
> Celuy qui meurt pour soy, & en mourant machine
> De tuer son tueur, void sa double ruine:
> Il void sa place preste aux abysmes ouverts,
> Satan grinçant les dents le convie aux enfers.

Misères, 1305:

> Les temples du payen, du Turc, de l'idolatre
> Haussent au ciel l'orgueil du marbre & de l'albastre;
> Et Dieu seul, au desert pauvrement hebergé,
> A basti tout le monde & n'y est pas logé!

Princes, 17:

> Car vous donnez tel lustre à vos noires ordures
> Qu'en fascinant vos yeux elles vous semblent pures.

Princes, 505. The portrait of the ideal king is constructed out of contrasting moral qualities such as:

> Craintif en prosperant, dans le peril sans crainte

and

> Chiche de l'or public, tres-liberal du sien,

The speech of Fortune (*Princes* 1193–1318) to the innocent newcomer to court is contrasted with Virtue's speech (1335–1486). In advising the young man not to behave like the king's mignons, Virtue phrases her moral precepts in antitheses:

> Qu'ils prennent le duvet, toy la dure & la peine,
> Eux le nom de mignons, & toy de capitaine;
> Eux le musc, tu auras de la meche le feu;
> Eux les jeux, tu auras la guerre pour jeu.

At the beginning of *La Chambre dorée* there is a scene of apocalyptic wrath when God learns of the corruption of France. The reactions of Christians and sinners to the anger of God are contrasted:

> Le meschant le sentit, plein d'espouventement,
> Mais le bon le sentit, plein de contentement.

La Chambre dorée, 710. Picture of Moses.

> Prend en un poing l'espee, en l'autre les balances;

La Chambre dorée, 871:

> . . . la haute Majesté
> Les meine aux prisonniers cercher la liberté,
> Du pain aux confisqués, aux bannis la patrie,
> L'honneur aux diffamés, aux condamnés la vie.

La Chambre dorée, 964:

> Quand tu gardas ton ame en voulant perdre ame,

The fact that this is simply a translation of Matthew 16:25 does not detract from its stylistic importance. D'Aubigné welcomes paradox wherever he finds it. *Les Feux*, 209. Martyrdom of Lady Jane Grey:

> Un royaume est pour elle, un autre Roy luy donne
> Grace de mespriser la mortelle couronne
> En cerchant l'immortelle, & luy donna des yeux
> Pour troquer l'Angleterre au royaume des cieux:

This kind of contrast—the opposition of the divine to the worldly—is especially frequent in *Les Tragiques*. We have seen in our study of the Jacob's ladder motif how many of the grand theatrical scenes in the poem have a kind of two-story construction: on a lower level, historical happenings here on earth, and above, God and His angels in heaven. A few lines further on, the same princess is described as

> Prisonniere ça bas, mais princesse là haut,

And her last words are full of antitheses:

> Hay ton corps pour l'aimer, aprens à le nourrir
> De façon que pour vivre il soit prest de mourir,
> Qu'il meure pour celuy qui est rempli de vie,

In the scenes of martyrdom throughout *Les Feux* the poet exploits to the full the contrast of physical death and spiritual rebirth. Sometimes, as in the account of the execution of Marie d'Adrian, the antithesis is expressed in a single line:

> Ainsi la noire mort donna la claire vie,[43]

Montalcino's sermon at the stake, consisting as we have seen in an elaborate play on variations of the word "seul," comes to a climax in a passage entirely constructed of antitheses:

> O chrestiens, choisissez: vous voyez d'un costé
> Le mensonge puissant, d'autre la verité;
> D'une des parts l'honneur, la vie & recompense,
> De l'autre ma premiere & derniere sentence;
> Soyez libres ou serfs sous les dernieres loix
> Ou du vray ou du faux. Pour moy, j'ay fait le choix:
> Vien l'Evangile vray, va-t'en fausse doctrine!
> Vive Christ! vive Christ! & meure Montalchine![44]

43. *Les Feux*, 541.
44. *Les Feux*, 699–706.

In exhorting his fellow prisoners to die with him, Richard de Gastines insists on this same theme of the opposition between the false goods of this world and the true goods of heaven:

> Vous perdez le vray bien pour garder le faux bien,[45]

Elsewhere in the same speech, he says

> Aurez-vous liberté enchainans vostre cœur?

and

> Vous regardez la terre & vous laissez le ciel!
> Vous sucez le poison et vous crachez le miel!

This idea provides the occasion for innumerable antitheses in *Les Feux*. D'Aubigné's interest in the deaths of martyrs is readily understandable in view of the essentially propagandistic purpose of his poem, since these tragic episodes reinforce his argument; and of course an almost sadistic enjoyment of the horrible is evident in many passages of *Les Tragiques;* but there is also a stylistic reason for the poet's delight in such scenes. To a believer, the contrast between physical death and eternal salvation is the greatest and most dramatic of all antitheses. The death of a martyr provides almost endless opportunities for setting off truth against falsehood, God against the world, life against death. No more paradoxical situation could be contrived for the lover of contrasts.

The torment of Cain, fleeing from divine retribution, is another series of antitheses:

> Les lieux plus asseurés luy estoyent des hasards,
> Les fueilles, les rameaux & les fleurs des poignards,
> Les plumes de son lict des esguilles piquantes,
> Ses habits plus aisez des tenailles serrantes,
> Son eau jus de ciguë, & son pain des poisons; [46]

However, contrast receives its ultimate and most dramatic expression in the great Last Judgment scene in *Jugement*. Here the two magnificent speeches of God to the elect and to the damned are, line for line, in direct antithesis, like the two sides of a medieval tympanum:

Lines 871–876:

> Vous qui m'avez vestu au temps de la froidure,
> Vous qui avez pour moy souffert peine & injure,
> Qui à ma seche soif & à mon aspre faim
> Donnastes de bon cœur vostre eau & vostre pain,

45. *Les Feux*, 751.
46. *Vengeances*, 203–207.

> Venez, race du ciel, venez esleus du Pere;
> Vos pechés sont esteints, le Juge est vostre frere;

Lines 886–891:

> Vous qui avez laissé mes membres aux froidures,
> Qui leur avez versé injures sur injures,
> Qui à ma seche soif & à mon aspre faim
> Donnastes fiel pour eau & pierre au lieu de pain,
> Allez, maudits, allez grincer vos dents rebelles
> Au gouffre tenebreux des peines eternelles!

The sensibility of the modern intellectual may lead him to ascribe a wholly symbolic value to Last Judgment scenes; to do so, however, is to misunderstand d'Aubigné. To so staunch a believer the contrasts between earthly vanities and everlasting judgment are more than mere rhetorical antitheses; they are actually contrasts between illusion and reality. Furthermore, to a mind which views the world as divers et ondoyant, the difference between seeming and being is a never-failing source of interest. It is natural, therefore, that the theme of *disguise* should be important in the poetry of d'Aubigné; and it seems appropriate, at this juncture, to move on to a consideration of this problem.

7. DISGUISE

The world of *Les Tragiques* is one of disguises. Everywhere, false appearance is contrasted with truth. It may almost be said that d'Aubigné's chief intention in writing his poem is to unmask the wicked. He is constantly demonstrating that, under an outward show of power and magnificence, the rulers of France are really cruel, corrupt, and weak. Above all, to this militant Protestant, the Catholic Church is really the devil in disguise. But, while d'Aubigné is undoubtedly sincere in his desire to lay bare wickedness in high places, this moral mission does not preclude a keen intellectual pleasure in the contrast between seeming and being. Since the baroque mind does not see the world in self-evident, logical, Cartesian terms, it is dramatically aware of this conflict between illusion and reality and feels that if paradox and complexity did not exist, the world would be a less interesting place.

As one might expect, the book of *Princes* is good hunting ground for the unmasking of surprises. The poet explains that it is his duty to tell the truth about corruption in the government; if he attempted to whitewash his princes, he would be as wicked as they are:

> Des ordures des grands le poëte se rend sale
> Quand il peint en Cesar un ord Sardanapale,

Quand un traistre Sinon pour sage est estimé,
Desguisant un Neron en Trajan bien-aimé,
Quand d'eux une Thaïs une Lucrece est dite,
Quand'ils nomment Achill'un infame Thersite,[47]

D'Aubigné's indignation against poets who flatter the monarch is undoubtedly genuine—he may even have had Ronsard in mind—but the reader will, I think, feel that this passage betrays a certain interest in disguise for its own sake. The poet has been able to indulge his taste for comparing truth and appearance. However, court poets are not the only persons to be blamed for disguising truth: court preachers are equally wicked:

> . . . en chaire les flatteurs
> Portent le front, la grade, & le nom de prescheurs:
> Le peuple, ensorcelé, dans la chaire esmerveille
> Ceux qui au temps passé chuchetoyent à l'oreille,
> Si que, par fard nouveau, vrais prevaricateurs,
> Ils blasment les pechez desquels ils sont autheurs,
> Coulent le moucheron & ont appris à rendre
> La loüange cachee à l'ombre du reprendre,
> D'une feinte rigueur, d'un courroux simulé
> Donnent pointe d'aigreur au los emmiellé.[48]

These various techniques arouse d'Aubigné to mingled feelings of moral indignation and intellectual gratification. First of all, there is the preacher who hypocritically praises the behavior of a vicious king. (This variety of intellectual dishonesty has, of course, always been particularly prevalent in funeral sermons.) Often the priest in the pulpit is himself guilty of the very sins which he is ostensibly denouncing—a paradox which emphasizes the contrast between appearance and reality. Finally, in preaching before the king, some religious orators employ the ingenious technique of attacking a minor foible of the monarch in order to cover up a major crime which passes unmentioned ("couler le moucheron"); in this way, there is an antithesis between the apparent and real intentions of the preacher who, seeming to criticize, is actually flattering. So we have in this passage a threefold disguise. But distortion of truth in the pulpit comes in for a more detailed censure:

> A-il pas tant cerché fleurs & couleurs nouvelles
> Qu'il habille en martyr le bourreau des fideles!
> Il nomme bel exemple une tragique horreur,
> Le massacre justice, un zele la fureur; [49]

47. *Princes*, 89–94.
48. *Princes*, 123–132.
49. *Princes*, 137–140.

Although as a moralist and a Protestant d'Aubigné has an intense hatred for Catholic orators who try in this way to justify persecutions and massacres, as an artist he almost admires the skill which is capable of creating such illusions. The baroque, it should be remembered, is frequently an illusionistic art; Borromini's colonnade in the Palazzo Spada alla Regola and Bernini's Scala Regia in the Vatican are both exceedingly clever pieces of delusive perspective, made to appear many times their actual length. Similar in technique are the flat ceilings of churches painted by Pozzo to look like domes, and the false shadows so often adopted by baroque fresco painters in an attempt to give the impression that the light is coming, not from a natural source, but from heaven. To all this, in stern disapproval of an art that glorified Catholicism, d'Aubigné would probably have exclaimed (as he does with respect to the court preachers):

> Voilà comment le Diable est fait par eux un ange![50]

and yet, being himself an artist of similar sensibilities, he would have felt a secret admiration for the technique which made such illusionistic feats possible.

Henri III's fondness for carnival masquerades is looked upon as a form of disguise, indulged in to cover up the massacres of his reign:

> Bizarr'habits et cœurs, les plaisants se desguisent,
> Enfarinez, noircis, & ces basteleurs disent:
> "Deschaussons le cothurne et rions, car il faut
> Jetter ce sang tout frais hors de nostre eschaffaut,
> En prodiguant dessus mille fleurs espanchees,
> Pour cacher nostre meurtre à l'ombre des jonchees."[51]

The general collapse of morality under the last of the Valois is also treated in terms of the disguise theme. According to the poet, in the good old days people called a spade a spade and recognized sin when they saw it, whereas his degenerate contemporaries use hypocritical euphemisms in order to cover up reality:

> Nos anciens, amateurs de la franche justice,
> Avoyent de fascheux noms nommé l'horrible vice:
> Ils appeloyent brigand ce qu'on dit entre nous
> Homme qui s'accommode, & ce nom est plus doux;
> Ils tenoyent pour larron un qui fait son mesnage,
> Pour poltron un finet qui prend son avantage;
> Ils nommoyent trahison ce qui est un bon tour,

50. *Princes*, 149.
51. *Princes*, 211-214.

> Ils appeloyent putain une femme d'amour,
> Ils nommoyent macquereau un subtil personnage
> Qui sçait solliciter & porter un message.[52]

Throughout, words are contrasted with facts and appearance with reality. Though there is no doubt in d'Aubigné's mind where reality lies, he is interested in the power of language to create misleading appearances.

I have already mentioned, in another connection, d'Aubigné's advice to sovereigns who really want to know what their subjects think of them: at court, truth is so obscured under flattery that the only thing for a wise prince to do is to assume a disguise and sneak around incognito, listening to what people say. This episode actually uses the disguise theme in two ways: first of all there are the hypocritical fawnings of the ruler's subjects, and then there are the borrowed garments worn by the ruler himself in his search for reality. A favorite word to express the idea of disguise is "fard" (cosmetics or make-up). The prince's purpose in disguising himself is to see "ses pechez sans nul fard"; and later, as he tests public opinion, he becomes "defardé du lustre de son vent" (incidentally, a mixed metaphor characteristic of the poet's multiple sense imagery).

It has been seen elsewhere that d'Aubigné, though himself prone to use erotic language in speaking of the love of God, disapproves of Catholics who do the same thing. Such poets are termed "rhymeurs hypocrites, Desguisez"[53] and also "Corbeaux enfarinez"—and thus the disguise theme is introduced once more.

Needless to say, Henri III's effeminate propensities—in particular, his habit of dressing up as a woman—receive prolonged and indignant attention. The description of "Sardanapale," wearing pearls in his hair and rouge on his face, has a considerable claim to historical accuracy; as the poet remarks, the French had

> En la place d'un Roy, une putain fardee.[54]

Aside from the moral aspects of the question, behavior of this kind presents a curious problem as to reality and appearance; d'Aubigné, torn between indignation and intellectual curiosity, wonders whether Henri III should actually be regarded as a man or as a woman:

> Si qu'au premier abord chacun estoit en peine
> S'il voyoit un Roy femme ou bien un homme Reine.[55]

52. *Princes*, 241–250.
53. *Princes*, 429–430.
54. *Princes*, 784.
55. *Princes*, 795–796.

In such a case, it is hard to decide which sex is an illusion and which a fact. The same problem, of course, arises with respect to the mignons:

> Ces hommes vont bravant des femmes l'ornement,
> Les putains des couleurs, les pucelles de gestes; [56]

Other court activities, no less reprehensible, are likewise carried out with the aid of disguises. We are already familiar with the carriage sent out from the Louvre in the middle of the night to kidnap a midwife and force her to perform an abortion on a masked queen:

> D'un coche qui, courant Paris à la minuict,
> Vole une sage femme, & la bande & conduit
> Prendre, tuer l'enfant d'une Roine masquee, [57]

The princesses, according to d'Aubigné, were in the habit of disguising themselves in order to go to work in bordellos:

> Nos princesses, non moins ardentes que rusees,
> Osent dans les bourdeaux s'exposer desguisees, [58]

And all the while the professional flatterers of the court cover up what is going on:

> . . . les plus subtils esprits
> A desguiser le mal ont finement apris
> A nos princes fardez la trompeuse maniere
> De revestir le Diable en Ange de lumiere. [59]

Because of the constant spectacle of vice cloaked in hypocrisy at court, the book of *Princes* provides the poet with the greatest opportunity of exploiting the disguise theme; but examples may be found in most parts of *Les Tragiques*, for the difference between seeming and being never fails to fascinate d'Aubigné. When, at the beginning of *La Chambre dorée*, Peace comes to plead before the throne of God she points out that the peaceful condition of France (in the interval between two of the religious wars) is only a false appearance, since under the surface persecutions, massacres, and guerrilla activities are constantly taking place:

> Fausse paix qui vouloit desrober mon manteau
> Pour cacher dessous lui le feu et le couteau,
> A porter dans le sein des agneaux de l'Eglise
> Et la guerre et la mort qu'un nom de paix desguise. [60]

56. *Princes*, 1070–1071.
57. *Princes*, 1029–1031.
58. *Princes*, 1011–1012.
59. *Princes*, 949–952.
60. *La Chambre dorée*, 75–78.

The image of the stolen cloak is characteristic.

To the Huguenot, Catholic ceremonies are simply a disguise which camouflages wickedness. Everything Catholic priests do is a fraud; there is no truth behind their outward show of piety. With this idea, we are still in the midst of the illusion-reality problem. So when d'Aubigné describes an auto-da-fé we again find the disguise theme; the martyred victims of the Inquisition march by with devils painted on their costumes:

> . . . Les heritiers insignes
> Du manteau, du roseau & couronne d'espines
> Portent les diables peints: les Anges en effect
> Leur vont tenant la main autrement qu'en portraict;
> Les hommes sur le corps desployent leurs injures,
> Mais ne donnent le ciel ne l'enfer qu'en peinctures.
> A leur dieu de papier il faut un appareil
> De paradis, d'enfers & demons tout pareil.
> L'idolatre qui fait son salut en image
> Par images anime & retient son courage,
> Mais l'idole n'a peu le fidele troubler,
> Qui n'en rien esperant n'en peut aussi trembler.[61]

In this scene, appearance and reality are exactly reversed; for the Protestant martyrs, who seem to be covered with devils, are actually being led by angels; and the Catholic priests, who make such an outward show of religious authority, are really fraudulent deceivers who have no contact with God. The Protestant hatred of graven images (evidenced in England also by Cromwell's soldiers) is well known; and throughout *Les Tragiques* d'Aubigné speaks with approval of those who destroy Catholic "idols" or trample upon the Host. Like Montaigne, he was well aware of the dangerous power of the imagination. The *Apologie de Raymond Sebond* cites numerous examples to show how men's ideas are influenced by irrelevant and external things: the sound of martial music makes us courageous in battle; the robes of a judge make us think that he is wise. Pascal, when he advised the man in search of religious faith to go through the outward gestures of religious devotion, was conscious of the same problem. And so d'Aubigné mortally hates and fears Catholic ritual, because he feels that it may lead men away from the "true" religion. Thus the question of the relationship between illusion and reality was, for all these men, a vital one. Montaigne, deeply interested in the illusions created by our senses and imagination, concluded that, because of them, we have no "communication à l'estre" and cannot arrive at truth without divine assistance. Pascal, influenced by Montaigne, recognized the "puissances trompeuses" but felt that the power of ritual to act upon the imagination could be made to serve

61. *La Chambre dorée*, 549–560.

the cause of religion. Now d'Aubigné was very willing to use incarnational imagery in his poetry when he felt that it would aid in the expounding of Protestant doctrine; but for precisely the same reason, knowing the power of physical symbols, he was afraid of idolatry when practiced by Catholics. When it suits his own purpose, appearance has a symbolic correspondence with reality; used by his adversaries, appearance is dangerous and misleading. So it is that in *Les Feux,* speaking of those who persecuted John Huss and Jerome of Prague, he refers to

> Ceux qui n'estoyent pasteurs qu'en papier & titres.[62]

Since the Catholics are, in d'Aubigné's mind, noteworthy for their deceits and disguises, it is not surprising that Satan himself is distinguished by the same characteristics. When in a scene from *Les Fers* which is reminiscent of the Book of Job, Satan comes before God to ask permission to tempt and torture the faithful, he has masked his true nature, and appears as an angel:

> Il n'esblouït de Dieu la clarté singulière
> Quoiqu'il fust desguisé en ange de lumiere
> Car sa face estoit belle & ses yeux clairs et beaux,
> Leur fureur adoucie; il desguisoit ses peaux
> D'un voile pur & blanc de robes reluisantes;
>
> Ainsi que ses habits il farda ses propos,[63]

(Note again the typical verb "farda," of which the poet is so fond.) Here the cleavage between illusion and reality is brought to its climax: disguise is felt to be an attribute of the devil himself. When Satan, having obtained the desired permission, descends to earth, he makes continual and effective use of disguise:

> Tantost en conseiller finement desguizé
> En prescheur penitent et homme d'Eglise
> Il mutine aisément, il conjure, il attise
> Le sang, l'esprit, le cœur & l'oreille des grands.
> Rien ne luy est fermé, mesme il entre dedans
> Le conseil plus estroit. Pour mieux filer sa trame
> Quelquesfois il se vest d'un visage de femme,
> Et pour piper un cœur s'arme d'une beauté.
> S'il faut s'authoriser, il prend l'authorité
> D'un visage chenu qu'en rides il assemble,[64]

And there follows a list of other disguises. Sometimes the devil assumes the shape of a hypocritical monk wreathed in rosaries, or of a barefoot mendicant

62. *Les Feux,* 65.
63. *Les Fers,* 41–45 and 48.
64. *Les Fers,* 214–223.

friar; at other times he dresses himself as a judge; finally, he often turns himself into gold to tempt man's avarice.

D'Aubigné's preoccupation with disguise is in itself a paradox and reveals a curious inner tension. The Protestant and the poet are in conflict. The religious moralist feels that there is something essentially satanic about disguise; the baroque artist delights in the contrast between being and seeming.

8. METAMORPHOSIS

D'Aubigné's world is not only one of surprise and disguise: it is also a world of transformation and metamorphosis. His conception of reality is not static but dynamic; as the Germans would say, he is interested in "Werden"; like Montaigne, he paints not "l'estre" but "le passage." Presumably this Protestant poet believed that God is unchanging, but almost everything else in *Les Tragiques* undergoes agitated change. The poem might be compared to a moving picture rather than to a still photograph; whenever possible, objects are presented to us not in fixity and repose but in motion and transformation. This characteristic is evident on almost every page, and is so important a feature of d'Aubigné's poetry as to constitute a fundamental orientation of his mind.

A poem describing the religious wars of the sixteenth century is necessarily much concerned with bloodshed. Indeed, nearly every river in *Les Tragiques* is red with blood. But d'Aubigné generally chooses to depict not the static quality of redness but the *change to redness*. The following quotation will illustrate what is meant:

> . . . mais les ondes si claires
> Qui eurent les sapphirs & les perles contraires
> Sont rouges de nos morts; . . .[65]

It is the transformation that counts here. By emphasizing that the "ondes" were once "claires" the poet has impressed us chiefly with a moving picture of a change in color. The metamorphosis of water into blood is also one of the crimes of Catherine de' Medici: she

> Tourne la terre en cendre, & en sang l'eau changee.[66]

During the Massacre of St. Bartholomew, the Seine

> Tient plus de sang que d'eau; son flot se rend caillé,
> A tous les coups rompu, de nouveau resouïllé
> Par les precipités: . . .[67]

65. *Misères*, 62–64.
66. *Misères*, 898.
67. *Misères*, 871–873.

It is not just that there is a lot of blood in the river; the water is continually
being stirred up and stained by the bodies thrown into it. Similarly, the cities
on the Loire, such as Orléans,

> Troublent à cette fois Loire d'un teint nouveau,[68]

In such scenes d'Aubigné is really painting "le passage" rather than "l'estre."
But of course wars bring many other transformations. When, in *Misères*,
the poet compares the French nation to a diseased giant, he dwells upon the
changes wrought by illness on the body:

> Ce grand geant changé en une horrible beste
> A sur ce vaste corps une petite teste,
> Deux bras foibles pendans, des-ja secs, des-ja morts,[69]

As a result of war and famine, even domestic animals have turned into wild
beasts:

> De ces evenemens n'ont pas esté exclus
> Les animaux privez, & hors de leurs villages
> Les mastins allouvis sont devenus sauvages,[70]

The adjective "allouvis," "transformed into wolves," which is of frequent
occurrence in *Les Tragiques,* shows that the poet is interested not merely in
the fact that animals and people are fierce but that they have *become* so.
    In the midst of the disaster which has overtaken France, Nature herself
seems to be degenerating:

> Quand Nature sans loy, folle, se desnature,
> Quand Nature mourant despouille sa figure,[71]

It is, of course, far more terrifying to watch things getting worse and worse
than just to observe that they are bad; that is why d'Aubigné, always eager to
strike horror into the hearts of his readers, chooses to present his subject in
this dramatic form.
    Old age is described in terms of the changes it brings:

> . . . la caducque vieillesse
> Qui nous oste l'ardeur & nous croist la finesse,[72]

The Protestants, in their prayer to God at the end of *Misères,* compare themselves to the Catholics; the passage presents a contrast between two metamorphoses:

68. *Les Fers,* 1071.
69. *Misères,* 157–159.
70. *Misères,* 464–466.
71. *Misères,* 485–486.
72. *Misères,* 665–666.

> Nous faisons des rochers les lieux où on te presche,
> Un temple de l'estable, un autel de lar cresche;
> Eux du temple un'estable aux asnes arrogants,
> De la saincte maison la caverne aux brigands.[73]

Given this basic idea—that the Protestants, having no churches, are obliged to worship in barns, while the Catholics, in their fine churches, are arrogant, ignorant, and blasphemous—it seems to me characteristic of d'Aubigné that he has elected to stress the idea of *transformation,* so that we seem to witness not a static condition but an evolution. And when this feature is combined with a sharp antithesis, I think we have a passage which is unmistakably baroque.

In the idea of salvation, d'Aubigné is interested in the progressive transformation of the soul. Man, when he first glimpses divine truth, is filled with enthusiasm; then

> L'enthousiasme apprend à mieux cognoistre & voir
> De bien voir le desir, du desir vient l'espoir,
> De l'espoir le dessein, & du dessein les peines,
> Et la fin met à bien les peines incertaines.[74]

Thus the saving of the soul is a dynamic process. On the other hand, the happiness of the wicked will fade away:

> Les delices des grands s'envollent en fumee [75]

The souls of wicked flatterers are ever changing:

> Et vostre ame, flatteurs, serfve de vostre oreille
> Et de vostre œil, vous meut d'inconstance pareille
> Que le cameleon: . . .[76]

In other words, the faithful are steadily evolving toward salvation, while the sinners are in a constant state of flux—neither are in fixed repose but both are undergoing change.

Later, d'Aubigné returns to his physiological metaphor of comparing France to a diseased body; the infection is still growing worse:

> Quand la playe noircit & sans mesure croist,
> Quand premier à nos yeux la gangrene paroist,[77]

Not only does sexual perversion exist at court, it is constantly spreading; corruption and jealous squabbling become more and more prevalent:

73. *Misères,* 1317–1320.
74. *Princes,* 179–182.
75. *Princes,* 217.
76. *Princes,* 233–235.
77. *Princes,* 475–476.

> Et le vice croissant entre les compagnons
> Brisa l'orde amitié, mesme par les ordures,[78]

The downfall of Henri III is enthusiastically foretold. The poet derives a vindictive pleasure in prophesying the disaster of an enemy, but he also is fascinated by the metamorphosis of a king into a corpse:

> Ces corbeaux se paistront un jour de ta charogne,[79]

Strange to say, even ignorance is dynamic rather than static:

> Elle est le chaud fumier sous qui les ords pechez
> S'engraissent en croissant s'ils ne sont arrachez,[80]

When Virtue, indignant at the immoral advice which Fortune is giving to the young and inexperienced courtier, expels her from the boy's bedroom, we have a dramatic transformation scene:

> La mere et les enfans ne l'eurent si tost veuë
> Que chascun d'eux changea en demon decevant,
> De demon en fumee, & de fumee en vent,
> Et puis de vent en rien. . . .[81]

The importance of sorcery has already been discussed; the characters of *Les Tragiques,* living in an agitated, demoniacal world, are forever being bewitched, changing their forms, or vanishing. The supernatural is a poetic theme congenial to d'Aubigné not only because it arouses fear but also because it lends itself to scenes of transformation.

In describing the building materials of the Palais de Justice, the poet has combined horror and metamorphosis:

> Mais Dieu trouva l'estoffe & les durs fondemens
> Et la pierre commune à ces fiers bastimens
> D'os, de testes de morts; au mortier execrable
> Les cendres des bruslez avoyent servi de sable,
> L'eau qui les destrempoit estoit du sang versé;
> La chaux vive dont fut l'edifice enlacé
> Qui blanchit ces tombeaux & les salles si belles,
> C'est le meslange cher de nos tristes moëlles.[82]

The atmosphere is that of a gruesome fairy tale, in which wicked sorcerers turn human beings into stones and mortar. Although the passage is actually only a metaphor, we have the feeling that d'Aubigné would like us to take it

78. *Princes,* 870–871.
79. *Princes,* 988.
80. *Princes,* 1089–1090.
81. *Princes,* 1328–1331.
82. *La Chambre dorée,* 179–186.

seriously and that he himself is not far from believing in this diabolical metamorphosis. And when, a little further on, we read that the evil judges sleep

> Sur des matras enflez du poil des orphelins [83]

we are almost ready to believe it literally.

Among the allegorical figures which inhabit the law courts Vengeance is represented as a steadily growing, dynamic force:

> . . . la Vengeance au teint noir, palissant,
> Qui croit & qui devient plus forte en vieillissant? [84]

Even the innocent victims of the law courts are viewed dynamically, as seeds which will transform themselves into the garden of Zion:

> Les cendres des bruslez sont precieuses graines
> Qui, apres les hyvers d'orage et de pleurs,
> Ouvrent au doux printemps d'un million de fleurs
> Le baume salutaire, & sont nouvelles plantes
> Au milieu des parvis de Sion fleurissantes. [85]

This concept recurs a number of times elsewhere, notably in *Les Feux*: d'Aubigné looks upon martyrdom as a germinating force which will transform the world. The Protestant victims will, by their heroic example, win converts to the new religion; their death will cause new life to grow. In the passage just quoted the image is developed to its extreme limits: the ashes of the martyrs are considered as seeds and their blood becomes an irrigating stream which will help the plants grow.

The evil influence of Catherine upon the French government is described in terms of metamorphosis: the lilies of France have been transformed into the golden balls of the Medici pawnshop coat of arms:

> Quand on verra les lis en pillules changer, [86]

However, a day of reckoning will come, when the wicked judges are swept away:

> Juges, sergens, curés, confesseurs & bourreaux,
> Tels artisans un jour, par changemens nouveaux,
> Metamorphoseront leurs temples venerables
> En cavernes de gueux, les cloistres en estables,
> En criminels tremblans les senateurs grisons,
> En gibet le Palais & le Louvre en prison. [87]

83. *La Chambre dorée*, 219.
84. *La Chambre dorée*, 331–332.
85. *La Chambre dorée*, 654–658.
86. *La Chambre dorée*, 775.
87. *La Chambre dorée*, 879–884:

D'Aubigné visualizes the punishments to be visited on the wicked as consisting essentially of *degenerations*.

There is also a statement in *La Chambre dorée* which reminds one of Montaigne's famous, already mentioned "Le monde n'est qu'une branloire perenne." D'Aubigné, in reflecting that even Protestant England may some day come to know the evils of corrupt law courts, remarks:

> . . . il n'y a rien sous le haut firmament
> Perdurable en son estre & franc du changement.[88]

Just as Montaigne was struck by the endless mutability of human moods, so d'Aubigné makes one of his infant martyrs cry out at the stake:

> L'homme est si inconstant à changer de demeure,
> La nouveauté lui plait; & quand il est au lieu
> Pour changer cette fange à la gloire de Dieu,
> L'homme commun se plaint! . . .[89]

The importance of the concept of germination and the poet's fondness for the seed-and-growth metaphor to express the manner in which martyrdom will win converts have been observed. When Marie d'Adrian, in *Les Feux*, sees the coffin which has been prepared to receive her body, she is probably thinking of her own resurrection rather than the spiritual influence which her example will exert upon the witnesses of her death; nevertheless, the idea of germination is present:

> C'est, ce dit-elle, ainsi que le beau grain d'eslite
> Et s'enterre & se seme afin qu'il ressuscite.[90]

The Roman victims of papal persecution are also scattered seeds:

> Oui, le ciel arrose ces graines espanduës
> Les cendres que fouloit Rome parmi les rues: [91]

The ashes of the martyrs, scattered to the winds, will be more vital than the bodies of their persecutors, buried in marble tombs:

> Leurs cendres qu'on jetta au vent, en l'air, en l'eau
> Profiteront bien plus que le puant monceau
> Des charognes des grands, que morts, on emprisonne
> Dans un marbre ouvragé: le vent leger nous donne
> De ces graines partout: l'air presqu'en toute part
> Les esparpille, & l'eau à ses bords les depart.[92]

88. *La Chambre dorée*, 943–944.
89. *Les Feux*, 954–957.
90. *Les Feux*, 534.
91. *Les Feux*, 1181–1182.
92. *Les Feux*, 67–72.

Martyrdom appears as a great biological force, and the spread of Protestantism is likened to the growth of plants in nature.

The author's grim gratification at the spectacle of divine retribution in *Vengeances* is, as previously remarked, the natural desire of the member of an oppressed minority to see his tormentors destroyed—the same psychological urge which makes d'Aubigné take intense delight in the Book of Revelation. But it is interesting to note that the poet imagines the wrath of God as manifesting itself principally in disastrous transformations. Along with his mingled feeling of vindictiveness and self-righteousness, he takes much pleasure in the metamorphoses for their own sake:

> Terre, qui sur ton dos porte à peine nos peines,
> Change en cendre & en os tant de fertiles plaines,
> En bourbe nos gazons, nos plaisirs en horreurs,
> En soulfre nos guerets, en charongne nos fleurs.[93]

In the same scene he calls upon the waters to destroy the earth by flood:

> Eaux qui devinstes sang & changeastes de lieu,

and the air also undergoes a sinister change:

> L'air fut obeissant à changer ses douceurs
> En poison, . . .

In *Vengeances,* city after city is turned into ashes. In fact, as long as this earth still subsists all will be turbulent transformation. Only after the Last Judgment will stability be established; but the Judgment itself is represented as one last giant metamorphosis:

> Le grand moteur fera, par ses metamorphoses,
> Retourner mesmes corps au retour de leurs causes.
>
> Ainsi le changement ne sera la fin nostre,
> Il nous change en nous mesme & non point en un autre,
> Il cerche son estat, fin de son action:
> C'est au second repos qu'est la perfection.
> Les elemens, muans en leurs regles & sortes,
> Rappellent sans cesser les creatures mortes
> En nouveaux changements: le but & le plaisir
> N'est pas là, car changer est signe de desir.
> Mais quand le ciel aura achevé la mesure,
> Le rond de tous ses ronds, la parfaicte figure,
> Lors que son encyclie aura parfait son cours
> Et ses membres unis pour la fin de ses tours,
> Rien ne s'engendrera: le temps, qui tout consomme,

---

93. *Vengeances,* 285–288.

En l'homme amenera ce qui fut fait pour l'homme;
Lors la matiere aura son repos, son plaisir,
La fin du mouvement & la fin du desir.[94]

This passage is an appropriate conclusion to any consideration of metamorphosis as a theme in the poetry of d'Aubigné. Here we clearly see that, for the author of *Les Tragiques,* agitated change is the normal condition of all earthly things; the world will be "divers et ondoyant" until the Last Judgment. Growth, decay, germination, and metamorphosis will go on until the universe is destroyed. Only in paradise will relief be found from desire (which is an aspect of change) and from the perpetual fluidity of all things.

We have sought, in this study of paradox and mutability, to define some of the essential characteristics—with regard to both form and content—of *Les Tragiques.* For this purpose it has seemed desirable to furnish many examples from the text of the poem. From these illustrations the reader will probably be led to realize that the world of d'Aubigné is not reasonable, static, or classical.

As a religious man d'Aubigné longs for unity, but he sees everywhere a host of contradictions, surprises, and changes. Perhaps no logical system can be devised to explain reality in unified fashion. Everything is different from everything else; nothing is what it seems; and all things are in the process of changing their form. Montaigne, in the *Apologie,* while longing for absolute truth, arrives at the conclusion that man can have no "communication à l'estre" and ends, fideistically, with a faith based on skepticism. Montaigne and d'Aubigné were, temperamentally, very different men; but one is tempted to feel that it was the same basic sense of insecurity which led the one to moderation and tolerance and the other to a redoubled fanaticism.

From the point of view of poetic technique, d'Aubigné wholeheartedly enjoys devices that shock the reader's sense of logic and consistency: oxymoron, metaphoric antithesis, puns, surprise climaxes. As to subject matter, he is fond of describing startling contrasts, disguises, and metamorphoses. The poet is anxious to open our eyes to the complexity of reality. An artistic consciousness of the mutability of the world, combined at times with a desperate intellectual effort to find a unity which will give meaning to life, is an important aspect of the late sixteenth-century mind. The fact that d'Aubigné and many of his contemporaries—whether Catholic or Protestant—were striving, through force and religious faith, to impose order upon the world merely adds another paradox to the essentially paradoxical nature of the baroque spirit.

94. *Jugement,* 371–396.

Chapter V: BAROQUE ELABORATION:

An examination of two psalms, one adapted by Crashaw and the other by d'Aubigné, may help to shed light on certain characteristics of the baroque style. Richard Crashaw (1612–49) is now generally felt to be the most baroque of English poets: he excels in expressing by means of concrete and sensuous imagery states of agitated and ecstatic mysticism. His poems on Santa Teresa, in *Carmen Deo Nostro,* with their swooningly erotic conception of religion, form an interesting parallel to Bernini's sculptural group in the Roman church of Santa Maria della Vittoria, which shows Santa Teresa being rapturously pierced by the golden arrow of an attendant angel. For the moment, however, we shall be concerned with form and technique rather than with content and attitude; we shall compare, verse by verse, the King James Version of the Twenty-third Psalm with Crashaw's adaptation and try to see what devices of imagery and rhetoric appeal most strongly to this poet. In dealing thus with a text of established and well-known content, we can discern the peculiarities of the poet's manner.

On the other hand, Book III of *Les Tragiques, La Chambre dorée,* ends with an interesting paraphrase of Psalm 58. If we examine closely what d'Aubigné has done to this psalm, we shall (as in the case of Crashaw) get an idea of certain characteristics of his style; it is felt that these, also, will appear to be baroque.

Crashaw's rendition of Psalm 23 appears in *Steps to the Temple.* The King James text begins with the words:

1. The Lord is my shepherd; I shall not want.
2. He maketh me to lie down in green pastures: . . .

Now the poet's version of these lines:

> Happy me! O happy sheep!
> Whom my God vouchsafes to keep;
> Even my God, even He it is
> That points me to these paths of bliss;
> On Whose pastures cheerful Spring
> All the year doth sit and sing,
> And rejoicing, smiles to see

> Their green backs wear his livery;
> Pleasure sings my soul to rest,
> Plenty wears me at her breast,
> Whose sweet temper teaches me
> Not wanton, nor in want to be.

Several aspects of this passage deserve comment. The reader has probably already been struck by its length and elaboration as compared with the Bible text. It should be noted that the poem opens with two exclamations: "Happy me!" and "O happy sheep!" The abundant use of exclamatory sentences is typical of the baroque style, which is given to expressing religious feeling in terms of excitement and agitation. Significant, also, is the phrase "paths of bliss"; Crashaw, in common with Murillo and other baroque artists, emphasizes the voluptuous ecstasy of man's relationship to God. The word "Spring" has been reinforced by the use of the augmentative and perhaps superfluous adjective "cheerful." (As a matter of fact, the basic text makes no mention of season.) The green pastures have been described in a curious metaphor which, though not especially felicitous, is noteworthy: "Their green backs wear his livery." Again there is emphasis on sensuous delight in the line "Pleasure sings my soul to rest," and finally the passage concludes with a conceit on the words "want" and "wanton." We have observed, in our study of *Les Tragiques*, that d'Aubigné frequently introduces puns in highly serious passages where their use clashes with modern taste.

The Authorized Version text continues:

2. . . . he leadeth me beside the still waters.

This becomes:

> At my feet the blubbering mountain
> Weeping, melts into a fountain,
> Whose soft, silver-sweating streams
> Make high-noon forget his beams:

In his poem "The Tear" Crashaw has indulged in a similar elaboration of imagery. Mary's tear is compared to a watery diamond, a star, a drop of dew upon a rose, and so on. Here the single expression "still waters" has given rise to a lush heaping-up of images; the poet is playing with words that suggest wetness. Important, also, is the fact that in the King James text the waters are still, whereas in Crashaw's version this adjective has been replaced by others which suggest not repose but motion. Indeed, the whole landscape with its mountain and waterfall is a creation of the poet, reflecting a taste for picturesqueness, variety, and motion rather than static calm.

3. Bible: He restoreth my soul . . .

Crashaw:

> When my wayward breath is flying,
> He calls home my soul from dying,
> Strokes and tames my rabid grief,
> And does woo me into life:

Here again we have the use of augmentative adjectives—"wayward" and "rabid." The four lines, which replace four words of Bible text, are full of verbs which express motion and transformation: "flying," "calls home," "dying," and "woo." Thus the whole emphasis is on becoming rather than being; and while the idea may be implicit in the basic word "restoreth" Crashaw has certainly done everything possible to heighten the impression of evolution and movement. It is pertinent, also, to observe the use of words which suggest love-making: "strokes" and "woo." In this connection, it may not be far-fetched to reflect upon the possible secondary meaning implied in the word "dying." As Mr. Cleanth Brooks has pointed out the word had, in the seventeenth century, in addition to its usual sense that of experiencing the consummation of the act of love.

3. Bible: . . . he leadeth me in the paths of righteousness for his name's sake.

This is Crashaw's treatment of the theme:

> When my simple weakness strays,
> (Tangled in forbidden ways)
> He (my Shepherd) is my guide,
> He's before me, on my side,
> And behind me; he beguiles
> Craft in all her knotty wiles:
> He expounds the weary wonder
> Of my giddy steps, and under
> Spreads a path as clear as the day,
> Where no churlish rub says nay
> To my joy-conducted feet,
> Whilst they gladly go to meet
> Grace and Peace, to learn new lays
> Tuned to my great Shepherd's praise.

The scene has been converted into a sort of academic pastoral. Mr. Sypher has argued that certain paintings of Rubens, Poussin, and Claude Lorrain belong to what may be termed the "pastoral baroque"; to this tradition may also be assigned the minor poems of Milton, such as *L'Allegro, Il Penseroso,* and *Comus,* and the pastoral, précieux novel like *L'Astrée.* Whatever the merits of this theory may be, the reader must certainly be aware, in the Crashaw passage just quoted, of an elaborate and highly conventionalized pastoral atmosphere. The phrase "to learn new lays Tuned to my great Shepherd's praise" evokes an artificial world of courtly and sentimental shepherds and shepherdesses; Céladon comes more readily to mind than the Deity. Other stylistic alterations are worth noting: for example, the way in which "leadeth me" has been amplified into "expoundeth the weary wonder of my giddy steps." Crashaw's version, swollen by the addition of purely ornamental adjectives, appears distinctly précieux. With regard to the use of elaborate adjectives, "joy-conducted" is of a class with "silver-sweating," which appeared a little earlier in the poem.

4. Bible: Yea, though I walk through the valley of the shadow of death, I will fear no evil: . . .

Crashaw:

> Come now, all ye terrors, sally,
> Muster forth into the valley,
> Where triumphant darkness hovers
> With a sable wing, that covers
> Brooding horror. Come, thou Death,
> Let the damps of thy dull breath
> Overshadow even the shade,
> And make Darkness' self afraid;
> There my feet, even there, shall find
> Way for a resolvèd mind.

In the Bible text, there is just one concrete image—the valley of the shadow of death. In Crashaw's adaptation, we have not only the valley but also darkness hovering with a sable wing and the damps of the breath of death. To the visual picture of darkness has been added another sensation, pertaining to a different sense: dampness. A study of the rest of Crashaw's poetry reveals that not only is his imagery highly concrete but also it frequently appeals to several senses at once; his favorite adjectives, "sweet" and "delicious," as Mr. Austin Warren points out, mingle fragrance and taste. Indeed, this multiple sense imagery, so often met with in the poetry of d'Aubigné, and sometimes bordering on synesthesia, seems to be a favorite baroque device.

Crashaw has also made the scene highly theatrical. We have already noted the tendency toward the dramatic and spectacular repeatedly encountered in *Les Tragiques* and have mentioned the parallels in baroque art and architecture, such as the paintings of Rubens and El Greco, the ceilings for Roman churches executed by Pozzo, and the great baldachino of St. Peter's. It may be questioned, of course, whether Crashaw's overdramatization of the scene is really more powerful than the simple words "valley of the shadow of death"; but the poet's energetic efforts to make it so are incontestable.

One further rhetorical device should be noted here: the fondness for personification. The device has already been used in the preceding passage, where Grace and Peace appear; now, in addition, the poet calls upon "ye terrors," describes triumphant darkness as hovering with a sable wing, and refers to the damps of the dull breath of death. The abstract nouns are not only personified, they are adorned with a considerable amount of visual imagery and thereby endowed with individual life.

4 continued. Bible: . . . for thou art with me; . . .

Crashaw:

> Still my shepherd, still my God
> Thou art with me; . . .

4 concluded. Bible: . . . thy rod and thy staff they comfort me.

Crashaw:

> . . . still thy rod,
> And thy staff, whose influence
> Gives direction, gives defence.

Although these passages have undergone relatively little elaboration, certain stylistic peculiarities are present. Anaphora has been introduced by the threefold repetition of the word "still" and also in the line, "Gives direction, gives defence." These are, in reality, examples of the echo style, similar to those already discussed in *Les Tragiques*. The baroque, which in architecture enjoyed the effect of mass combined with movement, in poetry sometimes strove to achieve similar effects by various forms of repetition or accumulation. We have observed, in the poetry of d'Aubigné, the frequent use of asyndeton, which is essentially a heaping-up of words to attain massiveness; and we have also seen the extensive use of anaphora, or echoing of key words throughout a passage. Here the three clauses beginning with "still" and the two beginning with "gives" produce a general effect of heaviness. An impression of weight likewise comes from the substitution of the three words "influence," "direction," and "defence," for the single word "comfort."

5. Bible: Thou preparest a table before me in the presence of mine enemies: . . .

Crashaw:

> At the whisper of Thy word
> Crowned abundance spreads my board:
> While I feast, my foes do feed
> Their rank malice, not their need;
> So that with the self-same bread
> They are starved, and I am fed.

The commonplace table, presumably regarded as insufficiently elegant, has been replaced by "board"; and the presence of such words as "crown'd abundance" (incidentally, still another personification) and "feast" create an impression of lush gastronomy not found in the Bible text. Furthermore, the possibilities of contrast, inherent in the Authorized Version, have been more fully exploited. It has been observed that an interest in contrast as a rhetorical device and an inner psychological tension as a contradictory state of mind are everywhere present in the baroque. In this passage not only is my feasting contrasted with my enemies' starving, but also the literal and figurative senses of the word "feed" are set off against each other: "My foes do feed their rank malice, not their need." This particular kind of contrast, termed by Hatzfeld "veiled antithesis," is more traditionally known as syllepsis, and is frequently encountered in works of this period. It should be further remarked that the age of the Counter Reformation, being a time of religious conflict, is one in which artists, whether Catholic or Protestant as the case may be, seek to emphasize the victory of the faithful over their persecutors.

5 concluded. Bible: . . . thou anointest my head with oil; my cup runneth over.

Crashaw:

> How my head in ointment swims!
> How my cup o'erlooks her brims!

Direct statements have been transformed into exclamations and simple expression into hyperbole.

6. Bible: Surely goodness and mercy shall follow me all the days of my life: . . .

Crashaw:

> So, even so, still may I move
> By the line of Thy dear love;
> Still may Thy sweet mercy spread
> A shady arm above my head,
> About my paths; . . .

Perhaps the concept of goodness seemed too cold and abstract to Crashaw; at any rate, he has changed it to the warmer and more concrete idea of love. Love is further reinforced with the adjective "dear," and mercy with "sweet." Then, in order to adorn the idea still more, he has added the concrete image of one walking on a shady path. We have already commented upon Crashaw's fondness for the adjective "sweet" as combining the senses of taste and smell; note that here the multiple sense imagery, which constitutes virtual synesthesia, is carried still further by the use of "shady," which suggests coolness. The image of God's arm above the poet's head is, of course, in line with the baroque practice of expressing the love of God concretely and sensuously in terms of human love.

6 concluded. Bible: . . . and I will dwell in the house of the Lord for ever.

Crashaw:

> . . . so shall I find
> The fair centre of my mind,
> Thy temple, and those lovely walls
> Bright ever with a beam that falls
> Fresh from th' pure glance of Thine eye,
> Lighting to Eternity.
> There I'll dwell for ever, there
> Will I find a purer air,
> To feed my life with; there I'll sup
> Balm and nectar in my cup;
> And thence my ripe soul will I breathe
> Warm into the arms of death.

Once more, a single metaphor in the King James text has been expanded into a concrete and visual picture, as striking for richness and lushness as a canvass by Rubens. The profusion of terms suggesting brilliance and light should be noticed. Baroque art is, in its essential tendency, incarnational; and whenever painters of this period have sought to represent in visual terms God and heaven, they have created scenes of dazzling radiance. (Let the reader call to mind the supernatural light in certain pictures of El Greco and Murillo.) Crashaw, in his attempt to make us visualize the house of the Lord, employs the words "fair," "bright," "beam," "pure," and "lighting." We have already seen heaven depicted in similar terms in *Les Tragiques*.

As is so often the case, in building up his impression the poet has appealed to several senses at once. The images of light are followed by taste sensations ("there I'll sup Balm and nectar in my cup"); and the poem ends with feelings of almost erotic ecstasy: "And thence my ripe soul will I breathe Warm into the arms of death." This concept of the voluptuous death of the saint or martyr is constantly evident in baroque art, but perhaps nowhere with greater effectiveness than in Bernini's statue of the death of the Blessed Ludovica Albertoni. Thus the final note in Crashaw's rendering of the Twenty-third Psalm, like that of *Les Tragiques* itself, is one of trancelike swooning. The poem seems to open out sensuously into the infinity of God's love. I think that a parallel can be suggested here with Wölfflin's category of "open form" in baroque painting. The poem is not statically self-contained but suggests a limitless world beyond itself.

Let us now apply the same critical method to d'Aubigné's treatment of
Psalm 58 in the closing lines of *La Chambre dorée*. In making this comparison
we shall use the text of the Bible translated by the pastors and professors of
the Church of Geneva, which was published in 1588. While it is not certain
that d'Aubigné read the Bible in this text, it seems likely, in view of the date
of publication and the religion of the translators, to be reasonably similar to
any text he may have used. Lines 1011–1054 of *La Chambre dorée* correspond
to verses 2–12 of the psalm; the poet has devoted a stanza of four lines to each
verse of the Bible text.

Verse 2 of the psalm reads:

Mais de vrai vous gens de l'assemblee, prononcez-vous ce qui est iuste? vous fils
des hommes, iugez-vous en droiture?

D'Aubigné's version is:

Et bien! vous, conseillers des grandes Compagnies,
Fils d'Adam, qui jouëz & des biens & des vies,
Dites vrai, c'est à Dieu que compte vous rendez,
Rendez-vous la justice, ou si vous la vendez?

It will be noted that d'Aubigné has chosen to begin with a rather abrupt
exclamation. He has also given added weight to the interpellation by using the
reinforcing phrase, "qui jouëz & des biens & des vies." God's concern in earthly
affairs has been emphasized by the words: "c'est à Dieu que compte vous
rendez." We have had occasion to point out, in another chapter, how often
the scenes in *Les Tragiques,* like certain pictures by El Greco, are constructed
in two levels, human and divine. Perhaps the most significant device used in
this passage, however, is the sharply balanced antithesis in the last line:
"Rendezvous la justice, ou si vous la vendez?" The conceit provided by the
similarity between the two verbs serves to heighten the contrast; and actually
both verbs constitute an "echo" of "rendez" in the preceding line.

3. Ains vous brassez peruersité en vostre coeur: vous balancez la violence de vos
mains en la terre.

D'Aubigné:

Plustost, ames sans loy, perjures, desloyales,
Vos balances, qui sont balances inesgales,
Pervertissent la terre, & versent aux humains
Violence & ruine, ouvrage de vos mains.

Whereas the Bible text is content to address the judges as "vous," the poet
calls them "ames sans loy," and heaps upon them two opprobrious epithets,
"perjures" and "desloyales." In general, d'Aubigné's whole invective is much

stronger. The violent denunciations which appear all through *Les Tragiques,* such as, for example, the bitter diatribes against Catherine de' Medici, are justly celebrated; and M. Gonzague de Reynold has shown, in his *XVIIe Siècle,* that strong will, passion, and vitality are characteristics of the baroque mind. The heaping-up of powerful words to achieve a massive effect is seen not only in the epithets describing the evil judges but also in the doubling-up of "violence" and "ruine" in the last line. The anaphora in the second line serves the same purpose. Such a massing of vigorous words does not really add to the logical content, but it gives weight to the verse and creates the typically baroque impression of mass and movement.

4. Bible: Les meschans se sont estrangés dès la matrice, ils se sont forouyés dés le ventre de leur mere proferans mensonge.

D'Aubigné:

> Vos meres ont conceu en l'impure matrice,
> Puis avorté de vous tout d'un coup et du vice.
> Le mensonge qui fut vostre laict au berceau
> Vous nourrit en jeunesse & abeche au tombeau.

The Geneva pastors' version is, to be sure, concrete and physiological in its imagery, but the poet's adaptation has even greater brutality. This is partly because strong accents fall on the two verbs "conceu" and "avorté," which are contrasted with each other, and the second of which is introduced with the purpose of surprising and shocking the reader. D'Aubigné, like Crashaw, is fond of verbs which express transformation, change, or growth; note, for example, in the preceding stanza, the important position occupied by "pervertissent." The idea of giving birth can hardly be expressed in more violent form than by the verb "avorter," which is one of d'Aubigné's favorites. This word figures in a syllepsis, or "veiled antithesis," since it is employed both in a literal and figurative sense; the contrast between the two meanings is revealed in the words "vous" and "vice," both of which receive accents in the verse. The epithet "impure" heightens the invective. A supplementary concrete image, that of milk, has been added; the cradle and youth are contrasted with the tomb.

5. Bible: Ils ont du venin semblable au venin du serpent, & comme l'aspic sourd qui estoupe son oreille.

D'Aubigné:

> Ils semblent le serpent à la peau marquetee
> D'un jaune transparent, de venin mouchetee,
> Ou l'aspic embusché qui veille en sommeillant,
> Armé de soi, couvert d'un tortillon grouillant.

A l'aspic cauteleux cette bande est pareille,
Alors que de la queue il s'estouppe l'oreille:

In place of a simple simile, we have a pictorial and dramatic scene. The snake has become variegated in color; it is seen as lying in wait, writhing in coils. The exact manner in which the serpent stops up its ear—with its tail—is depicted. In the Bible text the simile merely serves the subordinate function of illustrating the idea; in the poem it is elaborated into a scene which strikes the eyes and exists for its own sake. With his love of contrast, d'Aubigné has insisted on the paradox of being awake and asleep at the same time. The echoed repetition of "aspic" should also be noted.

6. Bible: Lequel n'escoute point la voix des enchanteurs, du charmeur fort expert en charmes.

D'Aubigné:

Lui contre les jargons de l'enchanteur sçavant,
Eux pour chasser de Dieu les paroles au vent.

The essential antithesis contained in this simile—the idea that, whereas the serpent stops up his ears so as not to hear the snake charmer, the evil judges stop up theirs so as not to hear the voice of God—is certainly implicit in the Bible text; but in the poem it becomes explicit. Each of the two terms of the antithesis is stated in a full line; the Bible is content merely to suggest the second term. Curiously enough, in this passage a device which may ordinarily be considered as baroque has been abandoned by d'Aubigné: he gives up the echo of "charmeur" and "charmes."

7. Bible: O Dieu, casse-leur les dents en leur bouche. Eternel, rompts les dents maschelieres des lionceaux.

D'Aubigné:

A ce troupeau, Seigneur, qui l'oreille se bouche,
Brise leurs grosses dents en leur puante bouche;
Pren ta verge de fer, tracasse de tes fleaux
La machoire fumante à ces fiers lionceaux.

The reader will notice the augmentative adjectives and phrases with which d'Aubigné has decorated the text: "qui l'oreille se bouche," "grosses," "puante," and "fumante." But there is more to be observed about these than the bare fact that they add weight and emphasis. The repetition of "oreille" constitutes anaphora. "Puante" has been added for its shock value. Then, taken in consideration together with the preceding lines, this passage produces the familiar baroque effect of multiple sense impressions. The motley yellow color of the serpent strikes the eyes; next, sound is called upon, with the adder closing its ears to the enchanter's music; the sense of touch comes, rather violently, in the words "Brise leur grosses dents" and is suggested to a certain extent by the "verge de fer"; finally, smell is present in the stinking mouth. There is a play upon two different meanings of the word "bouche" and the last two lines are embellished with a quadruple alliteration: "fer," "fleaux," "fumante," and "fiers." While the Bible verse can hardly be considered a tranquil one, the poet has, by his choice of verbs, succeeded in stirring it up still more.

8. Bible: Qu'ils s'escoulent comme eau, & qu'ils le fondent: que chacun d'eux bande son arc, mais que ses flesches soyent comme si elles estoyent rompues.

D'Aubigné:

> Que, comme l'eau se fond, ces orgueilleux se fondent;
> Au camp leurs ennemis sans peine les confondent:
> S'ils bandent l'arc, que l'arc avant tirer soit las,
> Que leurs traits sans fraper s'envolent en esclats.

The images of fluidity and melting are already present in the basic text, so that no conclusion can be drawn from the poet's use of them; however, the echoing repetition of "fond" and "fondent" followed in the next line by the semipun of "confondent" is worth noting. The threat of enemies is certainly implicit in the Bible but d'Aubigné, unwilling to let slip so good an opportunity for using images of war, has explicitly mentioned both the camp and the enemy. The phrase, "Que leurs traits sans fraper *s'envolent en esclats,*" is both more visual in effect and more agitated in tone than "que les flesches soyent comme si elles estoyent rompues."

9. Bible. Qu'il s'en aille comme un limaçon qui se fond; qu'ils ne voyent point le soleil non plus que l'avorton de la femme.

D'Aubigné:

> La mort, dés leur printemps, ces chenilles suffoque
> Comme le limaçon dedans la coque,
> Ou comme l'avorton qui naist en perissant
> Et que la mort reçoit de ses mains en naissant.

Several new images have come to ornament this passage, although one (that of the sun) has disappeared. D'Aubigné has brought in the spring, has likened the judges to suffocating caterpillars, and has added the snail's shell. He has taken particular pleasure in emphasizing all possible contrasts: death is opposed to the spring, the abortion perishes the moment it is born, and death and birth are again contrasted in the last line.

10. Bible: Auant que vos chaudieres ayent senti le feu des espines, l'ardeur de colere ainsi qu'un tourbillon vous enleuera un par un comme de la chair crue.

D'Aubigné:

> Brusle d'un vent mauvais jusques dans leurs racines
> Les boutons les premiers de ces tendres espines;
> Tout pourrisse, & que nul ne les prenne en ses mains
> Pour de ce bois maudit rechauffer les humains.

Observe that this passage takes the form of an exhortation to God in d'Aubigné's version, rather than the future declarative sentence of the Bible text; this change results in an increased passion and vehemence. We have seen d'Aubigné's interest in images which express change, growth, decay, or transformation: these four lines are especially full of this theme. We begin with the complete burning of the thorns; then, going back in time, there is an allusion to the growth of buds into brambles; the exclamation "tout pourrisse" follows, and finally we have the verb "rechauffer" which itself expresses a change of state. It is not, I feel, exaggerated to argue that the concept of metamorphosis is present everywhere in this passage, as so often elsewhere in Les Tragiques. The presence of the adjective "maudit" is perhaps not significant here, but in the course of examining d'Aubigné's poem we have had occasion to see that he lives in a world of curses and enchantments, of demons and sorcerers.

11. Bible: Le iuste s'esiouïra quand il aura veu la vengeance; il lauera ses pieds au sang du meschant.

D'Aubigné:

> Ainsi faut que le juste apres ses peines voye
> Desployer du grand Dieu les salaires en joye,
> Et que baignant ses pieds dans le sang des pervers
> Il le jette en l'air en esclatant ces vers:

I think that we can see in this verse one reason why d'Aubigné was especially attracted to Psalm 58, so that he chose to paraphrase it as a triumphant conclusion to La Chambre dorée. The same note is struck here as throughout the Book of Revelation; and a cursory examination of the biblical sources of Les Tragiques will show that this is d'Aubigné's favorite book in the Bible. What the Huguenot poet enjoys in the Apocalypse is the vindictive and bloodthirsty character of its religious feeling. D. H. Lawrence has pointed out, in his interesting study of the Book of Revelation, that English dissenters, who so often belong to the downtrodden elements of the population, have always delighted in the prospect of that millennium, promised in the Apocalypse, when they shall be exalted and the rich and mighty tormented. Similarly, d'Aubigné, belonging to the faith of an oppressed minority, rejoices at those passages of Scripture which most violently foretell his bloody triumph over his enemies. One might suppose that there is little a poet can do here to embellish the already theatrical picture of the righteous bathing their feet in the blood of the wicked; however, a close examination of d'Aubigné's lines shows that he *has* succeeded in making the scene more agitated and more sadistic, for the "juste" is depicted as splashing the blood of the "pervers" into the air and bursting into song. Once again the Bible text has afforded the opportunity of developing an antithesis, since it speaks of rejoicing at vengeance, and the poet has made the most of his chance: "peines" are opposed to "salaires" and "joie," as well as "le juste" to "les pervers."

12. Bible: Et chacun dira, Quoi que ce soit il y a du fruict pour le iuste: quoi que ce soit il y a un Dieu qui iuge en la terre.

D'Aubigné:

> Le bras de l'Eternel, aussi doux que robuste,
> Fait du mal au meschant & fait du bien au juste,
> Et en terre ici bas exerce jugement
> En attendant le jour de peur & tremblement.

Here again the addition of an image, "le bras de l'Eternel," has made the passage more visually concrete and more dramatic. The "sweetness" of God, the attribute which seems to have appealed most strongly to Crashaw, is contrasted with His strength. *Les Tragiques,* while not lacking in passages which describe ecstatic swoonings, probably gives greater weight to the power and terror of God. It is so here, for the paraphrase of the psalm ends with fear and trembling. Compared with these four lines, verse 12 of the psalm is a relatively expository affirmation; d'Aubigné has insisted much more on the dramatic and emotional aspects of divine judgment.

In analyzing the adaptations which these two poets have made of their respective psalms, we do not intend to argue that the poems represent improvements over their originals; the reader will, in fact, very likely be led to feel the contrary. However, these texts have the advantage of being short and so of making it possible to examine, as in a microcosm, certain aspects of the poetic style of the late sixteenth and seventeenth centuries. These stylistic peculiarities have been analyzed, category by category, in our study of *Les Tragiques* as a whole; but here we may view them within a concentrated space.

It will be noted that many of the changes made in the psalms by Crashaw and d'Aubigné are in the direction of increased agitation, as when the former transforms still waters into a blubbering fountain, and the latter, not content with having the just bathe their feet in the blood of the wicked, makes them splash it into the air too. Other characteristics which the style of these two psalms seems to share in common with *Les Tragiques* as a whole, and with the art and architecture of the period, are: the love of elaborate, concrete imagery, often appealing to several senses at once; the use of contrasts and conceits; an interest in metamorphosis; and a frequent indulgence in theatricality. It is usually possible, in the smallest work of art, to discern the characteristics of an entire age. And so, if we have not quite, with Blake, seen eternity in a grain of sand, nevertheless much of the baroque has revealed itself in two psalms.

CONCLUSION

A STYLISTIC analysis of *Les Tragiques* reveals many analogies with the fine arts of the same period. These resemblances constitute a first reason for believing that d'Aubigné's poem, like the painting, sculpture, and architecture of the late sixteenth and early seventeenth centuries, belongs to the baroque style. Features which *Les Tragiques* shares in common with other contemporary works of art are: 1) an essentially propagandistic purpose, 2) a technique of exaggeration and overstatement, 3) a predilection for horrifying subjects portrayed with vivid and gruesome detail, 4) the prevalence of theatrical scenes, 5) the use of the *merveilleux chrétien,* particularly in "two-storied" theatrical scenes, 6) a fondness for the color red, often with an almost symbolic value expressing cruelty or violence, 7) the description of divinity in terms of radiant light, 8) multiple sense imagery, 9) a highly emotional, indeed frequently erotic, conception of the relationship between human beings and God.

Despite these parallels, Wölfflin's famous categories for distinguishing Renaissance and baroque art—a) linear vs. painterly, b) clear vs. unclear, c) multiplicity vs. unity, d) plane vs. recession, e) closed vs. open form—while setting up well-defined criteria for painting, sculpture, and architecture, do not appear to be applicable to literature. It might perhaps be argued that the closing passages of each book in *Les Tragiques* create an impression of opening out into infinity and that this aspect corresponds to "open form," but such comparisons are probably inaccurate and dangerous. How is one to discern, in the poetic description of a scene, what constitutes "plane" or "recession"? The difference between the media of the fine arts and literature is such that any attempt at adapting Wölfflin's criteria is likely to result in vagueness and imprecision.

I mentioned, in the Introduction, that the approach toward a definition of the baroque style would be inductive rather than deductive. Therefore, in reviewing here the various aspects of *Les Tragiques* discovered during the course of this investigation, my aim is to arrive at a synthesis. This reexamination raises again the question of the relative importance of form and content. In other words, have we merely been studying various devices of imagery and rhetoric which may perhaps be termed baroque, or have we gradually been discovering in d'Aubigné a certain way of looking at the world which may be called the baroque spirit? Actually, form and content, or style and spirit, can never be completely separated. An artist tends to use certain devices because they correspond to his vision of reality. This is true of any writer, even when he is copying traditional literary models or adopting conventions which happen to be fashionable at the moment; after all, the writer is a free agent and to employ a certain style implies a deliberate choice; if the style were not suited to the subject it would not have been chosen. This is all the more true of a man like d'Aubigné, whose poetry is no artificial literary exercise but the intimate expression of the experiences of his life.

If we reflect upon the characteristics which go to make up the style of *Les Tragiques,* we shall, I think, arrive at the conclusion that they may be grouped under two main headings—the *physical* and the *paradoxical.*

The physical includes those aspects studied in the first three chapters. Chapter I, it will be remembered, is entitled Energy, and consists of three subdivisions. The first of these, the Spirit of Propaganda, reveals the poet's readiness to impose his will by physical force if necessary; it corresponds to the warlike aspect of the poem. The second, Exaggeration and Emphasis, is connected with d'Aubigné's love of physical bigness and massiveness and decoration for its own sake. The final subheading, Horror and Martyrdom, analyzes his preoccupation with loathsome and shocking physical details. Chapters II and III—Spectacle and Incarnation respectively—are likewise devoted to the physical. In them we see the author's determination to act upon the reader's senses by physical means. These means are extremely varied—theatricality, the physical embodiment of the divine, the concrete expression of the abstract, the use of brilliant colors, imagery affecting sight, sound, hearing, smell, and taste simultaneously or in rapid succession—but in the end they possess one trait in common: their appeal is sensuous rather than intellectual.

The other main heading, the paradoxical, we have studied in Chapter IV: Paradox and Mutability; it includes those stylistic devices which proceed from a "divers et ondoyant" conception of reality: contrasts, surprises, disguises, and metamorphoses. These are more than superficial poetic tricks and correspond to a belief that the world is more complex than it seems, that reality has neither logic, unity, nor stability.

Thinking again of these two large divisions—physicalness and paradox—we find them to be related by one great resemblance and by one great difference.

Both in the *physicalness* and in the *paradox* of his poetry d'Aubigné rejects, a generation before the event, the Cartesian view of the world. By forever insisting on giving all ideas and feelings their most physical expression he shows that he dislikes intellectual abstraction: his mind is not a geometrical one. He enjoys physical sensations rather than ideas. Similarly, by insisting on the paradoxical, "divers et ondoyant" aspects of the world, the poet also repudiates the Cartesian, geometrical, unified view. There is an affinity between the love of sensations and the interest in the diversity of experience.

The two aspects of d'Aubigné's spirit, physicalness and paradox, present, however, an unreconcilable dichotomy. For the physicalness of *Les Tragiques* represents an attempt to give sensuous vividness to d'Aubigné's religious faith—through energy, spectacle, and incarnation d'Aubigné wishes to convert the reader to Protestant Christianity. D'Aubigné is actually striving to demonstrate the validity of his conception of God—in other words, to impose upon our minds a unified idea of truth. But this unified conception of the world is precisely what the other half of d'Aubigné's spirit cannot accept. The other half denies the possibility of a unified explanation of reality and actually delights in this diversity. There results a fundamental tension of the soul. It is perhaps in this tension that we may find the essence of d'Aubigné's style and spirit—and indeed of the baroque style and spirit.

It seems logical to assume that this tension of spirit was caused, in part at least, by the Reformation. We have seen that the baroque style cannot be limited to the Jesuit art of the Counter Reformation; however, the atmosphere of insecurity created by the schism of Christianity was probably a decisive factor in the formation of the baroque spirit. This schism not only aroused in Catholics and Protestants a fear of each other but gave rise to unconscious doubts as to the validity of Christianity itself. While the feeling of insecurity sometimes led to the skepticism of a Montaigne, it more often encouraged men to seek self-confidence through an increased religious fanaticism. Paradoxically enough, the *desire* to believe has perhaps never been stronger than in this age when belief began to be threatened.

It is thus clear that we feel the baroque to be more than a style; it appears to be the actual spirit of an age. This style and this spirit transcend the boundaries of individual arts (we have seen the affinities between *Les Tragiques* and baroque works of painting, sculpture, and architecture) and also international boundaries (for *Les Tragiques* has analogies with the poetry of Milton and Crashaw as well as with the painting of El Greco or the sculpture of Bernini).

It seems wise, however, to restrict the use of the term baroque to a specific historical period rather than to make of it a universal category. Those critics who have tried to extend the definition of baroque too far—such as Eugenio d'Ors—end by emptying it of all precise significance. The word, by coming to mean everything, means nothing. Inasmuch as the baroque in the fine arts is a definable historical era—say approximately 1550–1650—and inasmuch as literary parallels to the fine arts of this period can actually be discerned, it is preferable, with a few exceptions, to limit the literary baroque to the same period. One such exception might be Claudel's *Soulier de satin,* which after all deals with events occurring at the end of the sixteenth century.

Some critics may feel that the so-called baroque traits presented here may also be found in the Romantic era. This we feel to be a mistake because, though romantic poetry may often be violent, or theatrical, or rich in imagery, or full of antitheses, it presents, on one point, a significant difference. Romantic poetry is vastly more subjective than baroque poetry, vastly more concerned with expressing the author's personality and intimate life. This subjectivity, indeed, is carried so far as to result, frequently, in a self-identification of the author with the deity, whereas the baroque artist is always intensely aware of his own subordination to God. Furthermore, the baroque artist, by reason of his concern with paradox and the complexity of the world, realizes that, however much he may long to do so, he cannot through will reorder the world in his own image. The romantic artist is less likely to admit the importance of phenomena not in harmony with his will.

It would therefore appear prudent to require the presence of a great many, though of course not necessarily all, of the stylistic peculiarities enumerated in this book before admitting that a work is baroque. Concrete imagery alone, or antithesis alone, being devices which appear in every age, prove nothing. The simultaneous presence of a large number of these stylistic peculiarities, on the other hand, is usually significant. The critic must use his own judgment and not seek an infallible criterion. My own feeling, however, is that a literary work, in order to be accepted as baroque, should not only exhibit a considerable number of the stylistic traits discussed here but also should give distinct evidence of a dichotomy, in the author's spirit, between physicalness and paradox. The baroque writer is torn between the One and the Many; in so far as he believes in the One, he calls every physical means into play in order to impose upon the reader his particular vision of the One; in so far as he believes in the Many, he employs every device which will emphasize the surprises and picturesque diversity of the world. This fundamental inner conflict produces a profound restlessness which, quite as much as the elements of physicalness and paradox themselves, differentiates the baroque from the serenity, abstraction, and order of classicism. The classicist appears to feel that he has already achieved an orderly explanation of the universe; in his works he presents us with the finished product of his thought. The baroque artist, on the other hand, is still seeking, striving, and thinking as he writes. I hope that some of my readers may come to share my admiration for the picturesqueness, vitality, and *angoisse* of d'Aubigné's baroque.

BIBLIOGRAPHY

THROUGHOUT this study, the quotations from *Les Tragiques* are taken from the text of the Garnier-Plattard critical edition. Reproductions of the works of painting and sculpture mentioned may, for the most part, be found in Mâle or Weisbach; excellent photographs of buildings mentioned are to be found in Magni and in Fokker.

The most complete bibliography of the use of the term baroque in literary criticism from 1888 to 1946 is contained in Wellek's article, "The Concept of the Baroque in Literary Scholarship." A large number of the items on the following list are drawn from the Wellek bibliography. Listed here are those works which have been most valuable in the preparation of this book, or to which reference is made in the text.

D'Aubigné, A. *Œuvres complètes.* Réaume and de Caussade, eds. Paris, Lemerre, 1874.

———— *Les Tragiques.* Critical edition by A. Garnier and J. Plattard. Paris, Droz, 1932.

———— *Prose et poésie.* Anthology edited and with a preface by M. Raymond. Neuchâtel, Ides et Calendes, 1943.

———— *Le Printemps: L'Hécatombe à Diane.* Introduction by Bernard Gagnebin. Lille and Geneva, Droz, 1948.

Aury, D. *Poètes précieux et baroques du XVIIᵉ.* Introduction by Thierry Maulnier. Angers, Petit, 1941.

Babbitt, I. *The New Laokoon: an Essay on the Confusion of the Arts.* Boston and New York, Houghton Mifflin, 1910.

Boase, A. M. "Then Malherbe Came," *Criterion,* Vol. 9 (1930).

Boileau, N. *Œuvres.* P. Clarac, ed. Paris, Mellottée, n.d.

Brooks, Cleanth. *The Well-Wrought Urn.* New York, Reynal and Hitchcock, 1947.

Brosses, de, C. *Lettres familières sur l'Italie.* Paris, Ponthieu, 1799.

Crashaw, R. *The Poems.* J. R. Tuten, ed. London, Routledge, n.d.

Croce, B. *Storia dell'età barocca in Italia.* Bari, 1929.

Croll, M. W. "The Baroque Style in Prose," in *Studies in English philology; a miscellany in honor of Frederick Klaeber.* Minneapolis, University of Minnesota Press, 1929.

Donne, J. *The Poems.* Critical edition by H. J. C. Grierson. London, Oxford University Press, 1912.

Fokker, T. H. *Roman Baroque Art: the History of a Style.* London, Oxford University Press, 1938.

Hatzfeld, H. "Der Barockstil der religiösen klassischen Lyrik in Frankreich," *Literaturwissenschaftliches Jahrbuch der Görresgesellschaft zur Pflege der Wissenschaft im katholischen Deutschland,* IV (1929), 30–60.

———— *A Critical Study of the Recent Baroque Theories.* Bogotá, 1948.

———— "A Clarification of the Baroque Problem in the Romance Literatures," *Comparative Literature,* I (1949), 113–139.

Kohler, P. *Lettres de France, périodes et problèmes.* Lausanne, Payot, 1943. See chapter, "Le Classicisme français et le problème du baroque."

Loyola, St. Ignatius. *Spiritual Exercises.* Text in Spanish and English with commentary by Joseph Rickaby, S.J. London, Burns Oates and Washbourne, 1936.

Magni, G. *Il Barocco a Roma*. Turin, C. Crudo, 1911–13.

Mâle, E. *L'Art religieux après le Concile de Trente*. Paris, Armand Colin, 1932.

Montaigne, de, M. *Essais*. 3 vols. Critical edition by Villey. Paris, Alcan, 1922.

d'Ors, E. *Du Baroque*. Paris, Gallimard, 1935.

Plattard, J. *Une Figure de premier plan dans nos lettres de la Renaissance: Agrippa d'Aubigné*. Paris, Boivin, 1931.

Raymond, M. *Génies de France*. Neuchâtel, Editions de la Baconnière, 1942. See chapter on *Le Printemps*.

———— "Classique et baroque dans la poésie de Ronsard," *Concinnitas: Festschrift für Heinrich Wölfflin*. Bâle, 1944.

Reynold, de, G. *Le XVIIᵉ Siècle: le classique et le baroque*. Montreal, 1944.

Rocheblave, S. *Agrippa d'Aubigné*. Paris, Hachette, 1910.

Scott, G. *The Architecture of Humanism, a Study in the History of Taste*. New York, Scribner's, 1914.

Sponde, de, J. *Œuvres poétique*. Edition and preface by Marcel Arland. Paris, Stock, 1945.

Sypher, W. "The Metaphysicals and the Baroque," *Partisan Review*, XI (1944), 3–17.

St. Teresa, *The Life of St. Teresa, Written by Herself*. David Lewis, tr. London, 1888.

Vedel, V. "Den digteriske Barokstil omkring aar 1600," *Edda*, II (1914), 17–40.

Warren, A. *Richard Crashaw: a Study in Baroque Sensibility*. University, La., 1939.

———— "Edward Taylor's Poetry: Colonial Baroque," *Kenyon Review*, III (1941), 355–371.

Weisbach, W. *Der Barock als Kunst der Gegenreformation*. Berlin, Cassirer, 1921.

Wellek, R. "The Concept of Baroque in Literary Scholarship," *Journal of Aesthetics*, V (1946).

Wölfflin, H. *Renaissance und Barock*. Munich, 1888.

———— *Principles of Art History: the Problem of the Development of Style in Later Art*. M. D. Hottinger, tr. New York, Holt, 1932. (The first German edition, *Kunstgeschichtliche Grundbegriffe*, was published in Munich in 1915.)